PUT YOURSELF IN ...

PART II

Bible characters from the Acts, dramatically portrayed
for study, discussion and meditation

by Jane Archer

with illustrations by Brian Evans

For my grandchildren
Emily and Oliver Wickens – our 'young church'

CONTENTS

INTRODUCTION

...repentance bringing the forgiveness of sins is to be proclaimed
to all nations.
Begin from Jerusalem;
it is you who are the witnesses to it all.
(Luke 24:47-48 N.E.B.)

This was Jesus' last instruction to the disciples before his ascension, and arguably one of the hardest to comply with. They were told that all who had heard the Good News were responsible for spreading it to all who had not, throughout the world. This is a command which echoes down through the centuries but becomes no easier as time passes. Because it is a powerful undercurrent throughout the Acts of the Apostles, I have earmarked it as the theme of this volume.

In our twenty-first-century world, tolerance of other faiths and creeds has become the foundation stone for a peaceful society, and it is a quality which all of us struggle to build into our lives. So where does this put the words of Jesus? We are the new generation of 'witnesses to it all', so this is our responsibility. How should we implement Christ's command?

As I have ventured to suggest in other books of this series, a study of the men and women who first came into contact with Jesus and his teaching can often be helpful. How did they confront the issues, what problems did they face, what answers emerged? Needless to say, times and civilisations have changed, but sometimes the very differences give us fresh insights. And, of course, some situations are timeless, such that the behaviour of our characters from history may suggest patterns for our own way forward. What about the brotherly love of Ananias, who answered a cry for help with no regard for personal safety, or the generous spirit of Barnabas who allowed his leadership position to be taken by Paul and happily played second fiddle, or Priscilla who had the courage to challenge the accuracy of the distinguished speaker, Apollos?

Almost certainly, as we delve into the lives of the early disciples, we shall sense the prompting and power of the Holy Spirit which propelled their missionary efforts along, and sustained them when the going was tough. Perhaps this study will help us to depend on the power of the Holy Spirit more faithfully, and reflect it more effectively in our own lives.

This fourth book in the series forms the second of two parts dealing with the Book of Acts. Peter and others concerned with the Early Church in Jerusalem comprise the ten chapters of Part I; Paul and others featured in his journeys make up this second part. As in my previous books, each chapter begins with a dramatic speech or dialogue designed to bring the character to life. The words are imaginary, but each individual is carefully researched to discover as much as possible from the available evidence about these men and women from the past. Each portrait is further illustrated with a line drawing, the interpretation of which may itself prompt discussion. Four sketch maps record the routes taken by Paul and his companions. I hope that, by listening to the words and studying the material provided, the members of your group will not only learn more about themselves and each other, but will absorb something of the exuberance, vitality and comfort of the Holy Spirit which so empowered the early Christians in the service of their Saviour.

Practical tips for the use of the book

1. It is primarily intended for group use and is suitable for a wide range of ages, but can equally serve as a focus for private study. The character dialogues are useful bases for dramatic presentations in schools or in church services.

2. To achieve the greatest impact, the character dialogues should be acted, or read aloud. The use of local accents will add more colour and credibility to some, e.g. Lydia would probably have been upper class and possibly foreign, whereas the jailer's script hints at a Cockney accent.

3. Anachronisms and contemporary colloquialisms are used deliberately to make the character jump from the page and come closer to our own experience: for instance, Sergius Paulus makes the admission, 'I measured my length on the proverbial banana skin.'

4. The dramatic passages are followed by Bible extracts and references. Those printed in full give scriptural backing for much of the material in the dramatic script, and the leader is advised to use them with the group as they consider the character. This avoids preoccupation with details which are purely imaginary and less relevant to serious discussion. The

other Bible references may help to paint a wider background for the issues raised.

5. Next are some paragraphs of background notes, which highlight specific points in the material. They either paint a brief picture of places and people, or attempt to throw light on more complex issues. Of necessity, the notes are longer when they relate to particularly significant personalities of the Early Church.

6. Following the background notes, there are lists of discussion topics, each list being fairly long to allow a leader to make a selection appropriate to the group. Straightforward questions are included, together with others of a more searching nature to encourage growth of group fellowship through shared experience.

7. Each chapter ends with a prayer focusing on a theme from the material; some have been specially composed, others have been drawn from Scripture or from our Christian heritage.

8. It is important that members of the group understand clearly the imaginative nature of each dialogue. For some characters there is more material to lift from the Bible than for others. People should feel free to question the interpretations and make their own suggestions.

9. A bibliography at the end of the book offers guidance on source material.

ANANIAS

Hello there, friends! Come closer, I won't eat you! My name's Ananias, and I'm an easy-going sort of character – but a very ordinary one, let me stress that: no grand titles for me, no high position, no weighty responsibilities in Damascus. I'm just a respectable, God-fearing citizen who quietly goes about his business, and – top of my list – I'm one of the leaders of this new group of Jesus followers – or Followers of the Way, as we're usually called.

I mentioned Damascus – that's where I'm living. It's a great city – full of life, full of atmosphere, full of history; it's not as prestigious as it must have been centuries ago, but there's no doubt it has flourished under the Romans, and I love it! Travellers and traders pass through, and there's always something going on. Keep your ears flapping and you'll hear news from all the corners of the empire – particularly useful right now!

Having said that, it didn't dawn on me for a moment that the Lord God would single it out in quite the way he did – or single **me** out, I suppose would be more accurate. But then again, I guess that's why you've come to see me, so I'll tell you about it.

You must have heard about Saul, the young Pharisee from Tarsus, I'm sure … everyone has by now. Well, in the period before my extraordinary experience a month ago, it would be true to say we'd been hearing a new horror story every day about his sadistic activities in Jerusalem. I told you about the Followers of the Way, but I didn't explain that a group of us escaped from Jerusalem a while back to avoid the persecution that threatened everything. At that time it was fairly sporadic, but things deteriorated dramatically after the stoning to death of a preacher called Stephen. Saul supported the stoning, and seemed to see it as a green light for a personal orgy of persecution. From then on people all over Jerusalem were arrested and dragged from their houses. His brutality was the talk of this town, and everywhere else, no doubt. 'He's like a wild boar ravaging a vineyard', somebody said. So most of the remaining disciples fled the city then. Things were great here for a while, but then what happens? We hear Saul's heading for Damascus to use his heavy tactics here!

So that's the background for my story. As I mentioned, it happened about a month ago. We'd had a hectic day discussing how to handle this rumoured witch-hunt of Saul's – worrying, it was, because we knew the Lord's work must go on, but what if we were arrested? The thought of more hassle was frustrating and exhausting, and that night I know I was quite jumpy. I went to bed early, and, despite my anxiety, I must have dropped off almost at once. But sleep that night was clearly not on my schedule! In what seemed like no time, I was rudely awakened by a voice in my ear calling, 'Ananias!' I nearly fell out of bed with fright, it was so close. And yet what was quite peculiar was that, despite my dozy state, I knew at once that this was Jesus. 'Here I am, Lord!' I said and, can you believe it, he ordered me to go at once to a house in town where Saul was now staying. He'd apparently developed eye trouble on the journey here. I was to place my hands on his eyes, and that would bring his sight back! Imagine it! Put yourself in my shoes! This guy was intent on locking me up. Was it sensible to knock up the lion and offer myself on a plate in his den? When I could speak I muttered something about the frightening rumours we'd heard and the chief priests authorising Saul to round us up – that sort of thing. But believe me, the Lord is **amazing!** He just transforms everything and everybody.

He wasn't angry with my protest, just calmly explained that from now on Saul would be a key disciple, or something like that. He'd spread the good news – **Saul! Spread the good news!** Imagine it! – He would preach to kings and countries, and would even suffer for it. (I have to admit I approved of that bit!) So, of course, I did as instructed and – to cut a long story short – it all worked out as Jesus said. The strange thing is that, once I got going, I never doubted it. I was even feeling quite sympathetic towards Saul by the time I reached his place. I'd never actually seen him close before, and it was quite a surprise. The freaky-looking little blind man who greeted me looked **utterly** pathetic and I really did feel sorry for him. I remember calling him 'brother', which seems unthinkable! As I laid my hands on his eyes, weird scaly stuff fell off and he looked at me. I tell you, it was deeply, deeply moving and my instinct was to throw my arms round him. So when, after my suggestion, he agreed, 'Yes, baptise me now', I did it there and then. It seemed the most natural thing.

You just never know what's round the corner, do you?

BIBLE PASSAGES

Acts 9:1-19

In the meantime Saul kept up his violent threats of murder against the followers of the Lord. He went to the High Priest and asked for letters of introduction to the synagogues in Damascus, so that if he should find there any followers of the Way of the Lord, he would be able to arrest them, both men and women, and bring them back to Jerusalem.

As Saul was coming near the city of Damascus, suddenly a light from the sky flashed round him. He fell to the ground and heard a voice saying to him, "Saul, Saul! Why do you persecute me?"

"Who are you, Lord?" he asked.

"I am Jesus, whom you persecute," the voice said. "But get up and go into the city, where you will be told what you must do."

The men who were travelling with Saul had stopped, not saying a word; they heard the voice but could not see anyone. Saul got up from the ground and opened his eyes, but could not see a thing. So they took him by the hand and led him into Damascus. For three days he was not able to see, and during that time he did not eat or drink anything.

There was a believer in Damascus named Ananias. He had a vision, in which the Lord said to him, "Ananias!"

"Here I am, Lord," he answered.

The Lord said to him, "Get ready and go to Straight Street, and at the house of Judas ask for a man from Tarsus named Saul. He is praying, and in a vision he has seen a man named Ananias come in and place his hands on him so that he might see again."

Ananias answered, "Lord, many people have told me about this man and about all the terrible things he has done to your people in Jerusalem. And he has come to Damascus with authority from the chief priests to arrest all who worship you."

The Lord said to him, "Go, because I have chosen him to serve me, to make my name known to Gentiles and kings and to the people of Israel. And I myself will show him all that he must suffer for my sake."

So Ananias went, entered the house where Saul was, and placed his hands on him.

"Brother Saul," he said, "the Lord has sent me – Jesus himself, who appeared to you on the road as you were coming here. He sent me so that

7

you might see again and be filled with the Holy Spirit." At once something like fish scales fell from Saul's eyes, and he was able to see again. He stood up and was baptized; and after he had eaten, his strength came back.

Acts 22:12-16

"In that city was a man named Ananias, a religious man who obeyed our Law and was highly respected by all the Jews living there. He came to me, stood by me, and said, 'Brother Saul, see again!' At that very moment I saw again and looked at him. He said, 'The God of our ancestors has chosen you to know his will, to see his righteous Servant, and to hear him speaking with his own voice. For you will be a witness for him to tell everyone what you have seen and heard. And now, why wait any longer? Get up and be baptized and have your sins washed away by praying to him.'"

ADDITIONAL BIBLE REFERENCES FOR PRIVATE STUDY

Acts 7:54-60

Acts 8:1-3

BACKGROUND NOTES

1. Ananias

The Book of Acts tells of two other people by this name. One is the husband of Sapphira who sold property and tried to deceive the apostles about the sum of money it raised.

The other was a Jewish high priest before whom Saul (now called Paul) was tried after his third missionary journey.

The Ananias of this study was a respected Jew living in Damascus, who had become a believer before the time of Saul's visit. Not much is known about him since the only Bible references are the two passages already quoted, and since he does not feature significantly in the folklore and tradition of the period. He must have been known as a devout follower of Jewish Law since Saul alludes to this in Acts 22:12, his purpose being to show critics that strict Jews respected Ananias although he was a believer. Saul himself clearly regarded Ananias highly and spoke of him with affection. However, it is Ananias' unquestioning response to Jesus' call, and his supreme act of brotherly love in the face of personal danger, which have guaranteed him a place in the annals of Christianity.

2. Followers of the Way

The Early Church was known by this name until the people of Antioch in Syria invented the name 'Christian'. 'Followers of the Way' would seem an obvious choice on account of Jesus' frequent use of travel imagery with reference to himself. (*"I am the way, the truth and the life; no one goes to the Father except by me"*, *John 14:6*). The early believers no doubt saw life as a journey, with Jesus as the way to guide them through it.

3. Damascus

Damascus is situated about two hundred and forty kilometres from Jerusalem and has always played an important role as a centre of religion and commerce due to its strategic position at the crossing of trade routes. It was the ancient capital of Syria, and there is mention of it as far back as the sixteenth century BC. It was already well-known by the time of Abraham, and is frequently referred to in the Old Testament. Isaiah foretold its destruction *(The Lord said, "Damascus will not be a city any longer; it will be only a pile of ruins", Isaiah 17:1)*, and, indeed, it was finally conquered by the Assyrians in 732BC. They captured its treasures and many of its people, but fortunately the damage was not as complete as Isaiah's gloomy prediction. The city lost most of its prestige but continued to play a key part in trade and communications.

From 64BC to 33AD it was a Roman city. At the time of Saul's conversion there were numerous Jews living there in addition to the group of Early Church believers. Over the centuries the number of Christians in the population grew steadily, and a Christian community has continued there ever since.

The modern city of Damascus is once again the capital of Syria.

4. Stephen

Stephen was one of the seven Greek-speaking disciples of Jesus who were chosen by the Jerusalem apostles as deacons to assist in the distribution to needy widows, after a dispute had arisen between the Jewish and Greek-speaking groups of believers. He was known to be a man of great faith and charm, who was a powerful preacher and *'performed great miracles and wonders among the people' (Acts 6:8)*.

His vision of God's message being spread to the whole wide world was not what the Jews wanted to hear, and they engineered his arrest. On being dragged before the Sanhedrin, he responded to the string of trumped-up charges with a lengthy speech of defence outlining Israel's history, and demonstrating how God should not be limited to the confines of temples. It culminated in an accusation that the Jews were responsible for killing God's Son who was the prophet foretold by Moses.

He was stoned without a trial, but on the point of death stunned the onlookers with his appeal to God to forgive his killers.

The young Saul was present at the stoning, looking after the cloaks of the witnesses, and it was reported that he *'approved of his murder' (Acts 7:60)*. It would seem likely, however, that the experience played its part in his conversion.

5. Saul

The character of Paul forms a later chapter in this book, but a few words about his earlier years as Saul the Pharisee in Jerusalem are necessary to situate Ananias in the context of the narrative.

Luke regards Saul's conversion on the road to Damascus as such a stupendous occurrence in the history of the Early Church that he tells the story three times in Acts: once in its chronological place in the sequence of events, and twice more when the apostle defends himself before others. One of its most significant features was that Saul did not himself make a decision to follow Christ in the way that many people do, but rather it was Jesus who took the initiative and intervened in the life of someone we could only see as a most unlikely candidate for discipleship.

Saul had been brought up as a strict Pharisee, and all evidence suggests that his life's ambition was to devote his talents and energy wholeheartedly to the furtherance of Jewish laws and tradition. Far from experiencing twinges of guilt or uncertainty, he appears to have been proud of, and thoroughly satisfied with, his way of life. Rabbis viewed strict adherence to the law as essential for any hope of a Messiah, so it is easy to see why he would have no time for the followers of Jesus who were in every way a threat to the Jewish Establishment. It was at the time of Stephen's martyrdom that Saul's disapproval reached its zenith and he became a ruthless inquisitor, persecuting all connected with the early believers. He made house-to-house searches for Christians, and marched them off to prison, and when he discovered some had escaped the Jerusalem net, he persuaded the high priest to authorise a witch-hunt in Damascus. The Bible passages continue the story.

Scholars note that Luke refers to Saul here in language suggestive of wild animals rather than humans: for instance, in *'Saul tried to destroy the Church' (Acts 8:3)* the verb for 'destroy' is used in Psalm 80:13 of wild boars ravaging a vineyard; similarly in Acts 9:21 'killing' is translated from a verb suggestive of a lion mauling; finally the phrase *'kept up his violent threats of murder'(Acts 9:1)* is said to recall the snorting and panting of wild beasts.

So we can conclude that this conscientious, gifted, scholarly man was like a man possessed, crazed with hatred and fury such that he had the demeanour of a wild animal, as he set out on the road to Damascus.

DISCUSSION TOPICS

1. How does God make his will known to us?

2. Can you describe an occasion when your life as a Christian seemed to point you in an unexpected direction?

3. What do we mean by the term 'martyr'? What, if anything, do Stephen and suicide bombers have in common?

4. What sort of persecution exists in our society? How can we influence things?

5. When, if ever, is it right for us to judge other people? How should we handle others in our church family who are clearly disobeying Christian teaching?

6. How should we react to people of previously bad character who profess to have become Christians?

7. What do you find particularly difficult to forgive?

8. What does baptism mean to you?

PRAYER

Give me the faith which can remove
  And sink the mountain to a plain;
Give me the childlike praying love,
  Which longs to build thy house again;
Thy love, let it my heart o'erpower,
And all my simple soul devour.

My talents, gifts, and graces, Lord,
  Into thy blessèd hands receive;
And let me live to preach thy word,
  And let me to thy glory live;
My every sacred moment spend
In publishing the sinners' friend.

Enlarge, inflame, and fill my heart
  With boundless charity divine:
So shall I all my strength exert,
  And love them with a zeal like thine;
And lead them to thy open side,
The sheep for whom their Shepherd died.

Charles Wesley (1707-88)

BARNABAS

Christians! That's what they're calling us here in Antioch. What a great name! People say it's a taunt – they're taking the mickey – but why should we worry? It tells the world exactly who we are: 'Christ-followers'. What more do we want? I guess we'll have to see if it stands the test of time.

Talking of names, you'll be confused about mine, I guess? I'm a Jew from Cyprus and my name is really Joseph, but years ago the apostles decided I had to be Barnabas! For why, you ask. Very simple – there were several Josephs among the Jerusalem disciples at the time; Barnabas started as a nickname to identify me, and then stuck! I've always regarded it as a compliment, though, because it means 'encourager' and that's one of my aims in life. I can still picture what life was like at the beginning, and I'm going back upwards of fifteen years, now. We were a united group, the Jerusalem believers, in the very early days. We shared everything, ate together, supported each other, praised the Lord – everything seemed straightforward. Problems crept in later when converts flocked to join us from all over the place, but that's hardly surprising; we all had to get used to change. Early on, though, life was a doddle – and full of joy. I was fortunate enough to own some property, and I remember selling a field to boost our 'poor fund'. That was the money the apostles gave out if ever help was needed. It made you feel good, but, of course, it's what Jesus would have expected of us.

And then the persecution started and we were faced with new challenges. But then I thrive on challenge, you see. I'm a people-person, and God has directed me throughout several really testing situations. For instance, it was about ten years ago that I first rubbed shoulders with Paul, and I couldn't have done justice to that one without the Holy Spirit's guidance. Paul was only about two years into his ministry, and he'd come up against a solid brick wall. (Funnily enough, when I met up with him, he'd just escaped over one of those – literally – but that's another story!) You'll remember that Jesus had confronted Paul – or Saul as he was then – on the road to Damascus when he was set on persecuting believers everywhere. Paul responded to Jesus' call with all his might, talking with Jews and Gentiles alike, preaching in synagogues, proclaiming that Jesus was the Son of God – everything that the Spirit led him to do. But after about two years, pockets of resentment had built up, and a group of Jews plotted to murder him. They judged him a traitor to their cause and to the Jewish Law. That's when he had to escape over the city wall. He fled to Jerusalem to join the disciples there, but promptly met another hostility problem – understandable, when you think about it. He'd hounded them with his vicious persecutions – why trust him now?

That was **my** cue. I told them about his experience with Jesus, and all he'd been doing for our mission since. They were amazed to hear about his dynamic preaching and how people responded to it, and suddenly their hostility vanished. 'OK!' they said. 'You're on! Stay here with us and join the team!' That was trust indeed, and I was humbled by it. Only the Holy Spirit could bring about such a change, not any arguments of mine. But this is how he directs our lives, we know that. I've become even more aware of it since I've been here in Antioch. The Good News has taken root in fertile ground here, and Gentiles flock to be baptised. In fact that's what brought me here. The Jerusalem disciples were so rattled by the news of crowds of Gentiles joining the followers and moving the goalposts, that they sent me to find out what was going on. I'm not sure why me – I'm not known as a stickler for the Law and it was the Law they were concerned about, so stern discipline might have been the order of the day. Perhaps the moderates felt I'd be more useful chatting them round and keeping all the balls in the air; at least they were confident about my traditional background. So I saw it as a case for buckets of tact and diplomacy!

I couldn't have been more mistaken! The believers in Antioch were amazing! Overflowing with enthusiasm and adding to their number daily, they were full of the Holy Spirit and dedicated to his service. I didn't have to think 'What shall I do? How shall I handle this?', I just joined a group, rolled up my sleeves, so to speak, and got stuck in! Some were a bit worried about why I was sent from Jerusalem, but in no time we were trusted mates. I told them I hadn't seen commitment like it, the Lord would be well pleased with them.

'You're a tonic, Barnabas! You've spurred us on! You say such encouraging things!'

But what else could I have said? They were spreading the Good News to all and sundry just as Jesus instructed – and with such effect! The number of Gentile converts grew so vast that I needed help to manage everything. What we lacked was a powerful personality who could drive the project along. Yes, you've guessed it! I needed Paul! With him in charge the Antioch mission would forge ahead by leaps and bounds. It's strange that I should feel this way because when we're together people often take **me** for the leader, but Paul has the power and the charisma.

So that's what happened. I had to travel to Tarsus to track him down and persuade him, but we've been here together for over a year now. Things are going really well. Money for the work is flowing in so fast that someone suggested a collection to support poor believers in Judaea, and, Bob's your uncle, here we are setting off to deliver it!

BIBLE PASSAGES

Acts 4:32-37

The group of believers was one in mind and heart. None of them said that any of their belongings were their own, but they all shared with one another everything they had. With great power the apostles gave witness to the resurrection of the Lord Jesus, and God poured rich blessings on them all. There was no one in the group who was in need. Those who owned fields or houses would sell them, bring the money received from the sale, and hand it over to the apostles; and the money was distributed to each one according to his need.

And so it was that Joseph, a Levite born in Cyprus, whom the apostles called Barnabas (which means "One who encourages"), sold a field he owned, brought the money, and handed it over to the apostles.

Acts 9:19-28

Saul stayed for a few days with the believers in Damascus. He went straight to the synagogues and began to preach that Jesus was the Son of God.

All who heard him were amazed and asked, "Isn't he the one who in Jerusalem was killing those who worship that man Jesus? And didn't he come here for the very purpose of arresting those people and taking them back to the chief priests?"

But Saul's preaching became even more powerful, and his proofs that Jesus was the Messiah were so convincing that the Jews who lived in Damascus could not answer him.

After many days had gone by, the Jews met together and made plans to kill Saul, but he was told of their plan. Day and night they watched the city gates in order to kill him. But one night Saul's followers took him and let him down through an opening in the wall, lowering him in a basket.

Saul went to Jerusalem and tried to join the disciples. But they would not believe that he was a disciple, and they were all afraid of him. Then Barnabas came to his help and took him to the apostles. He explained to them how Saul had seen the Lord on the road and that the Lord had spoken to him. He also told them how boldly Saul had preached in the name of Jesus in Damascus. And so Saul stayed with them and went all over Jerusalem, preaching boldly in the name of the Lord.

Acts 11:20-30

But other believers, who were from Cyprus and Cyrene, went to Antioch and proclaimed the message to Gentiles also, telling them the Good News about the Lord Jesus. The Lord's power was with them, and a great number of people believed and turned to the Lord.

The news about this reached the church in Jerusalem, so they sent Barnabas to Antioch. When he arrived and saw how God had blessed the people, he was glad and urged them all to be faithful and true to the Lord with all their hearts. Barnabas was a good man, full of the Holy Spirit and faith, and many people were brought to the Lord.

Then Barnabas went to Tarsus to look for Saul. When he found him, he took him to Antioch, and for a whole year the two met with the people of the church and taught a large group. It was at Antioch that the believers were first called Christians.

About that time some prophets went from Jerusalem to Antioch. One of them, named Agabus, stood up and by the power of the Spirit predicted that a severe famine was about to come over all the earth. (It came when Claudius was emperor.) The disciples decided that they would each send as much as they could to help their fellow-believers who lived in Judaea. They did this, then, and sent the money to the church elders by Barnabas and Saul.

ADDITIONAL BIBLE REFERENCES FOR PRIVATE STUDY

Acts 13:1-5

Acts 13:49-52 and 14:1-28

Acts 15:1-21

Acts 15:36-40

BACKGROUND NOTES

1. Barnabas

Barnabas was clearly an attractive personality who made friends easily wherever he went, and had a happy knack of pouring oil on troubled waters. Luke interrupts his narrative to comment that Barnabas was a '*good man, full of the Holy Spirit*' – praise indeed in a piece of important historic writing which is concise – miserly, even – in its detail or comment. Theologians enthuse about his generous and godly character, and William Barclay calls him '*the man with the biggest heart in the Church*'. So what else do we know about him?

Barnabas was a Jew from the tribe of Levi, who came from Cyprus. He would have joined the Followers of the Way in the same period as Stephen and Philip, when the apostles were at the start of their mission of preaching and making converts. After the period in Antioch he accompanied Paul on his first missionary journey and was at first the leader of this expedition. After their return, at the Council of Jerusalem *(Acts 15)*, Barnabas defended the claims of the Gentile Christians with Paul. When Paul was about to set off on his second journey, the two parted company.

There is no further mention in the Bible of his activities but we know that he returned to Cyprus. He is credited with the founding of the Cypriot Church, and legend has it that he died as a martyr in AD61 at Salamis in Cyprus. Other tradition claims that he had earlier founded the Church of Milan and had been its first bishop.

The Christian writer Tertullian (160-225AD) attributed the writing of Hebrews to Barnabas for a variety of reasons, but the authorship of Hebrews has continued to be a talking point and a mystery.

With regard to physical appearance, we can assume that Barnabas had a commanding presence because the crowd at Lystra *(Acts 14:12)* likened him to the god Zeus, or Jupiter. Paul was likened to his son Hermes, or Mercury. Despite this implication that Barnabas was the leader, Luke draws attention to the fact that Barnabas himself asked Paul to lead, and seemed quite content to 'play second fiddle'.

2. Jews and Gentiles

From the introduction of Barnabas into the narrative, Luke's underlying theme becomes the inclusion of the Gentiles in the missionary work of the Church. At first, disciples had been telling the message only to other Jews

(Acts 11:19) but the rapid growth in Antioch bore witness to both aspects of the evangelism: there were synagogues in the city where much missionary preaching would have occurred, but we are told specifically about the additional involvement of the Gentiles *(Acts 11:20)*. Once again Luke is sparing with detail, writing that men from Cyprus and Cyrene took this momentous step of faith but omitting to tell us their identity.

3. Antioch

In the first century AD there were sixteen cities in the area named Antioch, two of which were visited by Barnabas and Paul. They were Pisidian Antioch in the heart of present-day Turkey, where the two men preached on the first missionary journey but were forced to leave after some Jews stirred up trouble *(Acts 13)*; and Syrian Antioch where Barnabas was sent to investigate the large numbers of converts. The latter is of particular importance in the growth of the Early Church, since it was here that huge revolutionary steps were taken in the evangelisation of non-Jews.

Syrian Antioch is the ancestor of the modern town of Antakya, on the Syrian border with Turkey. It was founded in about 300BC by Seleucus I Nicator who called it after his father or son, both of whom were named Antiochus. In Barnabas' time it was capital of the Roman province of Syria, and third city of the empire after Rome and Alexandria, boasting a population of over five hundred thousand inhabitants. Situated on the River Orontes with its own seaport, it was important both for commerce and for culture. It was renowned for the beauty of its buildings, particularly its long paved boulevard with double colonnade and fine landscaping, but it was also renowned for vice and immorality, and the magnificent pleasure park of Daphne was said to witness depravity of every kind. One can see why Barnabas might have been apprehensive about the Jerusalem disciples sending him to investigate goings-on in this colourful melting-pot of Western and Eastern cultures!

Antioch had a sizeable Jewish community, and after the stoning of Stephen, many believers fled there from Jerusalem, three hundred miles away. The groundwork was laid for one of the most active and important of the early Christian churches. It flourished for a long time second only to the Jerusalem church, but sadly, after being damaged by an earthquake in AD526, Antioch was sacked by the Persians in 540AD and the church never regained its status.

4. The name 'Christians'

As stated earlier, it was in Antioch that the believers were first called Christians. The name was a teasing or even contemptuous nickname, and it seems that the Antioch townspeople were known for their jokey nicknames: when the bearded Emperor Julian came to visit, they christened him 'the Goat'!

The believers must have used the title-word 'Christ' frequently in their teaching and preaching, referring to Jesus as 'the Christ', in the same way as he may be called 'the Messiah'. The coining of the name '*Christianoi*' was parallel to '*Herodianoi*' (Herod's people) and '*Kaisarianoi*' (Caesar's people).

The name 'Christian' did not, however, catch on quickly since there are not many mentions of it in the Bible, but it is ironic that a derisory name should then become the respected title for generations of believers.

DISCUSSION TOPICS

✓ 1. Why do you think church membership is declining in many places?

✓ 2. How important is the role of 'encourager'?

✓ 3. What makes people enthusiastic?

4. What do we mean by a person 'having charisma'? How is it acquired?

5. Barnabas was said to be full of the Holy Spirit – what signs can we see of that? What signs can be seen of the Holy Spirit in a) your home b) your church c) the wider world?

6. How true is 'Give a dog a bad name and hang him'? Have you seen this applied to anyone?

7. Do problems or divisions ever occur when newcomers join a church? If so, how are they resolved?

8. What is the value of mediation in human relationships? What makes a good mediator?

PRAYER

Dear God, we have been inspired by the example of Barnabas who used his talents so effectively in the Early Church.

We pray that you will show us how to play an equally vital part in the Church today. We ask you to give us the confidence to look for abilities within ourselves, and employ them energetically for your service.

> *Help us to have a positive attitude in all that we do, and to show it to those around us. May they know us as people who are quick to help in moments of need, and slow to criticise or condemn.*

> *Help us to work hard to solve problems, and offer mediation to those in conflict, so that tricky situations may be resolved and all parties are encouraged to begin things anew.*

> *Help us to bolster those whose confidence is shaken.*

> *Give us tact and diplomacy so that we blend comfortably with people, and are seen as enablers rather than antagonists.*

Above all, we pray that we may be filled with your Holy Spirit, so that our eyes sparkle with enthusiasm and our hearts overflow with your love. In this way may we draw people to your Kingdom. We ask this for Jesus' sake.

AMEN

Paul's first missionary journey

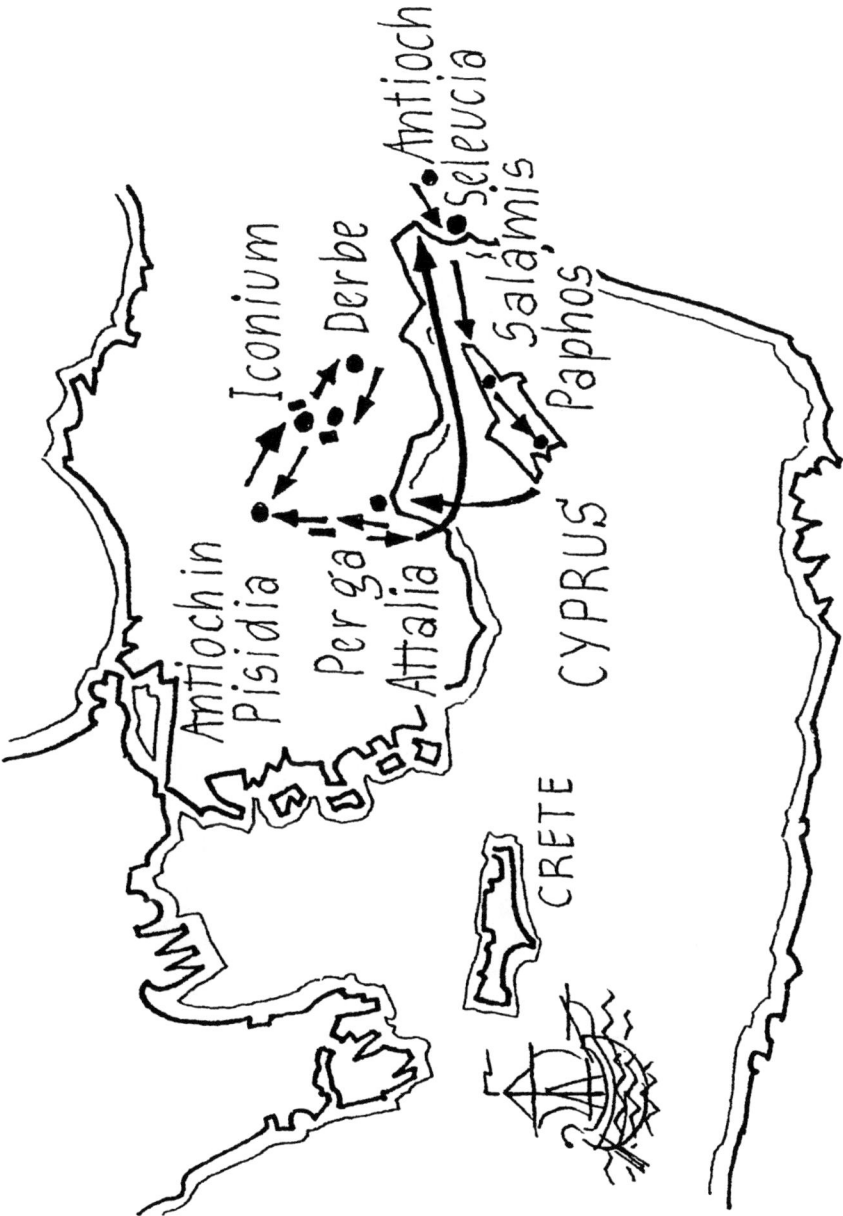

SERGIUS PAULUS

This is completely out of character, ladies and gentlemen – I have to admit that – and my words are for your ears alone . . . **strictly** confidential . . . as I'm making something of a confession to you.

Last week I found myself in an extremely embarrassing predicament, or as one might say, I measured my length on the proverbial banana skin. An undesirable individual insinuated his way into my confidence, and I fell for it. It is no exaggeration to say that I could well have compromised my position. Fortunately that is not the case, and I am here to tell the tale . . . a stronger man, hopefully, as a result of the experience.

I am Sergius Paulus, a proconsul of Rome, and I hold the much-respected post of governor of the Roman province of Cyprus. So imagine my mortification when I was shown publicly to be nurturing a viper in my retinue, to be putting my trust in an unscrupulous character who was out to manipulate me, if not worse. That would not be smiled upon by my superiors in Rome. If it were not for the fact that everything is thriving and prosperous here, and there is no whiff of the discord and skirmishing that disrupt many regions of the empire – indeed, if it were not for this evidence of satisfactory government (though I say it myself) then the situation might indeed be tricky for me. But this all goes to show we are living in strange times of revolutionary ideas and sudden change, and I, poor mortal, was caught unawares. At least I can console myself that good has come of the incident and we shall all benefit.

Enough of long-winded introduction and excuses! I will now lay the events before you as they occurred. You shall be the judges, but I would beg you to take due note of the important truth for all of us, which emerged at the encounter.

Until the day in question, I included in my retinue a Jewish magician called Bar-Jesus, or Elymas – he used two names, as is our custom. He was a learned and charming man, or so I thought, and he could always be relied upon to listen to my plans and offer his interpretation and predictions on the subject. You may not be aware of this, but it is customary for us Romans to keep such advisers in our households. You see, we respect the mighty power of the gods, and we are conscious of the need to avoid offence with our various policies and strategies for government.

I make no apology for the fact that I am a devout and conscientious governor. I care deeply for the welfare of my people here in Cyprus, and each decision involves me in much deliberation. Do you follow my drift? Yes, Elymas was at times my right-hand man. In the event of a crisis, I would summon him, and he would consult his charms and invariably come up with the answer. He was – or at least he **seemed** to be – a great philosopher, and often we would debate far into the night. When answers were not forthcoming, he would perform a few spells or incantations, and invariably all would be resolved. I encouraged this not only because I needed it, but also because it fascinated me. Where did these solutions, where did this power, come from?

The answer to my question was at hand, but very different from anything I might have expected. Three Followers of the Way had arrived on the island; I knew that as I had heard that they were making their way to my capital of Paphos from Salamis in the East, and that they were preaching in all the synagogues en route . . . apparently attracting much interest. I was intrigued – but a little suspicious, too, to be honest. I have no wish to see troublemakers disrupt the peace and all that we have worked for in this lovely province. 'Let me hear what they have to say,' I thought to myself, and so I sent for them. 'Come and explain to me this message from your God,' I ordered, and thereby opened the floodgates! I have never seen anything like it! There were three of them, two mature men – one tall and imposing, who seemed to be the leader, and one small but tough with gimlet eyes – and there was a young lad dancing attendance. They'd hardly crossed the threshold when Elymas, for no apparent reason, darted past me and blocked their path. He waved them back frantically as though they had a disease, and called over to me, 'These people have nothing to say to your Grace . . .' but that was as far as he got! What an uproar! **All hell** broke loose! The small fellow was like a man possessed. He fixed blazing eyes on Elymas, and positively annihilated him, accusing him of being the son of the Devil, of performing evil tricks, and of turning the truth of God into lies! I was appalled! At this stage I was confused as to where my loyalty lay. But worse was to come. And then there could be no mistake! The man – Paul was his name – called on his Lord to punish Elymas. 'Blind him, Lord!' he cried, and that's what happened . . . **instantly!** We were stunned, you could have heard a pin drop.

That settled things for me. A God with that sort of power is one to be reckoned with, believe me! I told you the power of the supernatural interested me, did I not? Well, I now mean to disregard people like Elymas, and concentrate on this Christian God. He is clearly the one to depend on!

BIBLE PASSAGE

Acts 13:1-12

In the church at Antioch there were some prophets and teachers: Barnabas, Simeon (called the Black), Lucius (from Cyrene), Manaen (who had been brought up with Herod the governor), and Saul. While they were serving the Lord and fasting, the Holy Spirit said to them, "Set apart for me Barnabas and Saul, to do the work to which I have called them."

They fasted and prayed, placed their hands on them, and sent them off.

Having been sent by the Holy Spirit, Barnabas and Saul went to Seleucia and sailed from there to the island of Cyprus. When they arrived at Salamis, they preached the word of God in the synagogues. They had John Mark with them to help in the work.

They went all the way across the island to Paphos, where they met a certain magician named Bar-Jesus, a Jew who claimed to be a prophet. He was a friend of the governor of the island, Sergius Paulus, who was an intelligent man. The governor called Barnabas and Saul before him because he wanted to hear the word of God. But they were opposed by the magician Elymas (that is his name in Greek), who tried to turn the governor away from the faith. Then Saul – also known as Paul – was filled with the Holy Spirit; he looked straight at the magician and said, "You son of the Devil! You are the enemy of everything that is good. You are full of all kinds of evil tricks, and you always keep trying to turn the Lord's truths into lies! The Lord's hand will come down on you now; you will be blind and will not see the light of day for a time."

At once Elymas felt a dark mist cover his eyes, and he walked about trying to find someone to lead him by the hand. When the governor saw what had happened, he believed; for he was greatly amazed at the teaching about the Lord.

ADDITIONAL BIBLE REFERENCES FOR PRIVATE STUDY

Acts 8:9-25 (Another magician confronted by the missionaries)

Isaiah 47:8-15 (The prophet warns against trusting magicians)

Matthew 24:23-25 (Jesus issues a similar warning)

BACKGROUND NOTES

1. First missionary journey

Paul's first missionary journey took about three years. Luke's report of it begins at Acts 13:3, where the church in Antioch blessed Paul and Barnabas and sent them, with John Mark, on their way to do the work commissioned by the Holy Spirit: they took the gospel to Cyprus and central Asia Minor, and it was there that Paul may have suffered ill health, possibly a virulent form of malaria. They eventually completed the trip, by which time several new churches had been founded.

2. The Holy Spirit

The authority of the Holy Spirit commands our attention three times in the few verses of Acts 13 describing the visit to Cyprus, and we are left in no doubt that he is the guiding force and inspiration behind the mission. As usual Luke is economical with detail, leaving us wondering how the Holy Spirit manifested himself, but the specific references to fasting, prayer and the laying-on of hands in verse 3 underline the significance of this commission. Here a Jewish 'false prophet' tries to thwart the Holy Spirit by preventing a Gentile – the governor – from hearing the gospel. God's power overthrows him and effects the conversion of Sergius Paulus.

So the start of Paul's first missionary journey moves his ministry forward from preaching to Jewish communities to direct evangelisation of Gentiles.

3. Cyprus

Cyprus, which had long been famous as a source of copper in the ancient world, became a Roman province in 58BC. There had been Jews on the island since the fourth century BC, and by the time of Paul's visit in 46AD they formed a substantial community throughout Cyprus. Barnabas, who originated from there, was an early convert to Christianity, so there were already believers on the island when Paul and his companions made this missionary journey.

They landed at Salamis which was the chief city before Roman times and also an important port, and then travelled about ninety miles across the island to Paphos, the administrative capital notorious for its worship of Venus, the goddess of love.

Governor of Cyprus must have been a popular posting as the island was sometimes called Makaria, the Happy Isle, on account of its perfect climate, prosperous economy and comparative freedom from discord.

4. Sergius Paulus

Little is known about Sergius Paulus apart from the Elymas incident in Acts 13, and he is not mentioned again in the Bible. An inscription records him as one of the 'guardians of the banks and Channel of the Tiber' during the reign of the Emperor Claudius, so this would probably have occupied him shortly before he became governor of Cyprus. His name is also featured in the writings of Pliny the Elder dating from about twenty years after this event, and also in the works of the third-century writer Galen. These references do little more than confirm his existence as an official of Rome, but reading between the lines of Luke's narrative, we can flesh him out a little.

He would have been posted to Cyprus for only one year. Outside Italy the Roman Empire had two types of province: peaceful ones, which were controlled by the Senate who appointed different governors, or proconsuls, each year; and unsettled ones which required troops to keep order. These came under the direction of the emperor, ruling via deputies, legates or procurators.

Sergius Paulus, as governor of a peaceful island, would have enjoyed a comfortable lifestyle and considerable prestige. His job was to keep order, administer justice, and collect the province's land and poll tax for transmission to the imperial treasury. It was not unknown for governors to abuse this last responsibility and line their own pockets, but there is no suggestion of corruption here. Sergius Paulus is described as intelligent, and seemed to be an approachable man who was sympathetic in his handling of the missionaries. He was happy to take advice from a personal trusted magician but this was a custom of the time rather than a particular sign of weakness.

5. Magicians

The early Christians were living in highly superstitious times, where dabbling in the supernatural was rife. People sensed unknown forces at work and inexplicable happenings in the world, so why not try magic for possible answers? Astrologers, soothsayers and magicians were a plentiful breed, and had considerable influence. Although frowned upon by Jewish prophets like Isaiah, they were generally respected in society, and widely used. Most were probably deluded and misguided 'do-gooders', rather than deliberate fraudsters or con men, but they undoubtedly made a comfortable living from their 'wares'.

They offered a variety of remedies such as amulets to charm away evil, magic bowls with curative inscriptions, spells and incantations, interpretation of dreams, astrology and a host of others. Clients came from all levels of society, and the Emperor Tiberius was said to have set the fashion for Romans by surrounding himself with private wizards.

Spells and incantations were used by – and even **devised by** – the great Solomon. The historian Josephus, in his *Antiquities,* describes a man being cured of demons through one of the King's remedies:

'The manner of the cure was this:- He put a ring that had a root of one of those sorts mentioned by Solomon to the nostrils of the demoniac, after which he drew out the demon through his nostrils; and when the man fell down immediately, he abjured him to return into him no more, making still mention of Solomon, and reciting incantations which he composed.'

Small wonder that the practice was popular and was deemed respectable by people like Sergius Paulus. Discrediting it undoubtedly created a major headache for the early Christian missionaries, thus giving Luke ample evidence for his account of the power of the Holy Spirit.

DISCUSSION TOPICS

1. What do you look for in a friend?

2. Can people in public life have genuine friends or advisers, or are they always vulnerable to pressure?

3. Is loyalty an outdated concept?

4. Do you read 'the stars' or other astrology tips in magazines etc.? If so, why? What sort of beliefs or fashions do people put their trust in nowadays?

5. What would have impressed Sergius Paulus about the missionaries and their message?

6. How would you try to explain the Holy Spirit to a) other church people and b) non-churchgoers?

7. Can you think of a person or situation you observed to be influenced by the Holy Spirit?

8. As church attendance is so low, how do people get to know about the gospel?

PRAYER

Dear Lord God, we thank you for your gift of friendship:
In times of happiness, we know that you are smiling with us
and sharing our joy;
In times of sadness, your words of comfort and reassurance light a candle
in our darkness;
In times of stress and anxiety, your strong arms hold us steady;
In times of anger and impatience, your voice of restraint troubles our
conscience and sets us on a better path;
In times of sin and error, your forgiveness is free and unconditional;
Most of all, Lord, we know that you are always there,
and will never let us down.

As we give you our thanks, we pray that we may be inspired to follow your
example of true friendship:
May we become for others the loyal friends who never change, the soul
mates whose love never dies, so that, with the help of your Holy Spirit, we
may all draw closer to the one whose love was so great that he lay down
his life for his friends, Jesus Christ our Lord.

AMEN

SILAS

Welcome, friends! I'm glad you've caught me, because I'm just packing my bag to sail off to Macedonia. Paul had this vision of some Macedonian chap urging us to go and help his people, so we plan to set sail in the morning. As you've probably gathered, Paul is not one to let the grass grow under his feet – although he'd say it was the Holy Spirit driving, not him. Between you and me, I've a hunch the Macedonian may be a disciple called Luke; he's opted to travel with us, and I think he hails from thereabouts. A young Christian called Timothy will also be joining us, so we're quite a party. I'll tell you about **him** in a minute.

My name is Silas, by the way. I'm an old stager of the church in Jerusalem. They call me a prophet, which means a sort of interpreter of the Law, I guess. I'm a Jew, of course – a Hellenist – and I've been fully involved at the church for years, teaching, preaching, writing, translating Greek, mediating in disputes, you name it! I have to say, though, this travelling around with Paul is a completely new experience for me. I'd have rated myself a bit long in the tooth for such adventures, but these past few months have been a real eye-opener. They've extended me spiritually, and enriched my discipleship. What a host of different people we've met . . . and so many clamouring to hear more about Jesus. It hasn't been all roses, of course; in one or two places we were decidedly *persona non grata*! – hardly surprising, when you consider how revolutionary our ideas are for some people. Guided by the Holy Spirit, we gave those a wide berth and journeyed on till we saw a friendly face.

One of the most memorable places for me was Lystra, an ancient town in Galatia whose inhabitants are a complete cocktail of different races. I mentioned young Timothy – he comes from there. The Romans took over the town around fifty years ago, so the rulers are Roman; education and trade seem to be in Greek hands, but the bulk of the population are from an obscure Anatolian tribe with their own dialect. Despite this they flocked to welcome us and communicate with us – it was thrilling. Paul said they treated him and Barnabas like gods on their last visit, till he sorted that one out! There is only a small Jewish community there, and Timothy's mother is one of them; she and her mother were both devout Christian Jewesses. His father was Greek. Everyone seemed to know Timothy, and they all spoke highly of him. I can see why. He's an appealing lad – not what you'd call tough, but firm in his faith and keen to put it into practice. He'll be a breath of fresh air for us oldies – I'm a great believer in having young people around. That's the teacher in me, you'll say!

One interesting thing came to light: Timothy had not been circumcised, I suppose on account of his Greek father, so Paul saw to that before we all left Lystra. He thought it desirable as we were special envoys of the Jerusalem church. And that reminds me – I didn't tell you the purpose behind my travelling. That all started with the subject of circumcision: at the end of their last journey, Paul and Barnabas gave a report to us at the church – all about their encounters, their preaching and the huge number of converts. We were delighted and praised God for the success of the mission, but there was a small group of the most rigid Pharisees who, as always, got really hot and bothered about such an influx of Gentile believers. You see, they're fanatical about the rules – and I can't blame them for that – but it does hinder the spread of the gospel which is our prime target. These Judaisers, as they're called, are adamant that everyone must be circumcised, and must follow the law of Moses but, of course, that all means nothing to our new brothers in Christ.

Fortunately our leader, James, is a profoundly wise and good man, whose judgement commands the respect of everyone. After much discussion he proposed that we should send a friendly letter to all the groups of new converts, welcoming them, apologising for any misunderstanding, and requesting that they abide by just a few conditions to do with things like food and moral behaviour. To make sure we all understood each other, he wanted two of our church leaders to accompany Paul and Barnabas, so they could hand over the letters in person. The strictest Pharisees would feel confident they'd convey the message fairly, and, of course, the local people would have someone there to explain things and answer any questions. That's where I came in, and I thank God for the privilege entrusted to me and the other leader, Judas Barsabbas.

My feelings were in turmoil as we set off! What a responsibility after all that had gone on. Would the people accept the conditions in the letter? I felt exhilarated, but distinctly apprehensive. Paul and Barnabas had told us enough about their hostile encounters for us to be under no illusions about the dangers we faced. Predictably, Paul was dismissive, convinced as ever that the Holy Spirit would see us through. And so he did! I was amazed at the delight of the Antioch people when they read the letter; I spoke with many, and they were enthusiastic, full of the Holy Spirit, and warm in their wishes of peace and blessing as we left.

The letter has now been delivered far and wide, and you can imagine the ripples of the Good News spreading through the world. What exciting times! I pray every day that the Lord's work will take hold and prosper like the seed on our farm land.

Meanwhile for us it's Macedonia and pastures new! Jesus said we were to be yoked up like the oxen to learn more about him so it was never going to be easy, was it? So long, friends!

BIBLE PASSAGES

Acts 15:1-2

Some men came from Judaea to Antioch and started teaching the believers, "You cannot be saved unless you are circumcised as the Law of Moses requires."

Paul and Barnabas got into a fierce argument with them about this, so it was decided that Paul and Barnabas and some of the others in Antioch should go to Jerusalem and see the apostles and elders about this matter.

Acts 15:22-35

Then the apostles and the elders, together with the whole church, decided to choose some men from the group and send them to Antioch with Paul and Barnabas. They chose two men who were highly respected by the believers, Judas, called Barsabbas, and Silas, and they sent the following letter by them:

"We, the apostles and the elders, your brothers, send greetings to all our brothers of Gentile birth who live in Antioch, Syria, and Cilicia. We have heard that some who went from our group have troubled and upset you by what they said; they had not, however, received any instruction from us. And so we have met together and have all agreed to choose some messengers and send them to you. They will go with our dear friends Barnabas and Paul, who have risked their lives in the service of our Lord Jesus Christ. We send you, then, Judas and Silas, who will tell you in person the same things we are writing. The Holy Spirit and we have agreed not to put any other burden on you besides these necessary rules: eat no food that has been offered to idols; eat no blood; eat no animal that has been strangled; and keep yourselves from sexual immorality. You will do well if you take care not to do these things.

With our best wishes."

The messengers were sent off and went to Antioch, where they gathered the whole group of believers and gave them the letter. When the people read it, they were filled with joy by the message of encouragement. Judas and Silas, who were themselves prophets, spoke a long time with them, giving them courage and strength. After spending some time there, they were sent off in peace by the believers and went back to those who had sent them.

Paul and Barnabas spent some time in Antioch, and together with many others they taught and preached the word of the Lord.

Acts 16:1-10

Paul travelled on to Derbe and Lystra, where a Christian named Timothy lived. His mother, who was also a Christian, was Jewish, but his father was a Greek. All the believers in Lystra and Iconium spoke well of Timothy. Paul wanted to take Timothy along with him, so he circumcised him. He did so because all the Jews who lived in those places knew that Timothy's father was Greek. As they went through the towns, they delivered to the believers the rules decided upon by the apostles and elders in Jerusalem, and told them to obey those rules. So the churches were made stronger in the faith and grew in numbers every day.

They travelled through the region of Phrygia and Galatia because the Holy Spirit did not let them preach the message in the province of Asia. When they reached the border of Mysia, they tried to go into the province of Bithynia, but the Spirit of Jesus did not allow them. So they travelled right on through Mysia and went to Troas. That night Paul had a vision in which he saw a Macedonian standing and begging him, "Come over to Macedonia and help us!" As soon as Paul had this vision, we got ready to leave for Macedonia, because we decided that God had called us to preach the Good News to the people there.

ADDITIONAL BIBLE REFERENCES FOR PRIVATE STUDY

Acts 15:3-21

1 Peter 5:12

BACKGROUND NOTES

1. Silas

Silas was a Hellenist Jew who was known by this name in the Jerusalem church where he was a prominent figure. He was also a Roman citizen, and in that context he would be known by the Latin form of his name, Silvanus. Roman citizenship was a privilege which was highly prized. It was part of Rome's policy of consolidating the empire to grant citizenship to certain select non-Romans, and it carried considerable perks: citizens had the right to vote, and they could not be imprisoned without trial. Neither could they be subject to scourging, which was the favourite way of extracting confessions. Finally, they had the right to appeal to Rome against any local heavy-handling they considered unjust.

What can we glean about Silas the person?

The elders of the Jerusalem church held him in high esteem as a scholar, church leader and diplomat, and for this reason they chose him (and Judas Barsabbas) for the crucial mission of delivering and interpreting a carefully-worded letter outlining the Church's conditions for acceptance of Gentile converts. Paul and Barnabas were instructed to take the letters on their next journey, but the two special envoys were to accompany them to spell things out and answer any questions. They obviously acquitted themselves well as the mission was accomplished cordially, and Silas remained on excellent terms with the people of Antioch.

Paul seems to have found him a good companion as they shared many crises together and Paul describes him as '*the faithful brother*' in 1 Peter 5:12.

Silas is generally thought to have been also a scholarly man, who assisted both Paul and Peter in the writing of certain New Testament letters. He was associated with Paul in the writing of his letters to the Christians in Thessalonica, and was almost certainly the scribe responsible for the writing of Peter's first letter. This contribution may well have been substantial, as the eloquent and scholarly Greek writing would be unlikely to have emanated from the pen of Peter himself. Some versions of the Bible still refer to the scribe of these letters by the Latin name Silvanus whereas others have substituted Silas throughout, for clarity.

We can conclude, therefore, that Silas was a good companion, a skilful diplomat, a natural leader and a gifted scholar. He is thought to have died in Macedonia.

2. Jerusalem Council 49AD

By the time Silas featured in the Acts story, the Early Church mission to the Gentiles had gained considerable momentum and crowds were being converted and baptised. Hitherto converts were absorbed into the community of the Jews by circumcision and by observing the Law, but now Gentiles were welcomed by baptism alone. So they were joining the Christian community without first becoming Jews. Strict Pharisees viewed this as a crisis situation: whilst they had come to accept that Gentile converts could learn God's ways and tread the Jewish path to salvation via circumcision and the Law of Moses, the laxity of this new situation seemed beyond the pale.

Acts 15 tells how the Jerusalem church called a council meeting to air these grievances and formulate policy for the future pursuit of God's mission. This meeting is regarded as a landmark in the evolution of the Church, since the main obstacles to Paul's – or rather the Holy Spirit's – mission to the Gentiles were finally swept aside, opening the way for further advance across the Empire.

3. James the Just

James, a brother of Jesus, was at that time leader of the Jerusalem church, and it was he who presided over this special council meeting. He was affectionately known as James the Just because of his outstanding moral leadership and conscientious adherence to the Law, and this meeting was no mean test of these qualities. Basically two main issues had been raised:

1. Were circumcision and obedience to the Jewish Law essential for salvation?

2. Could Jews socialise with Gentiles if Jewish rules for eating and personal behaviour were ignored?

At the end of the meeting James directed that the first of these be rejected. The Church's prime objective was to carry out God's instruction to preach the word to the Gentiles, and so no tradition from the past must be allowed to stand in the way of this mission. The strict Jews fared better on the second issue: by introducing the few fairly simple conditions outlined in the letter, James facilitated social interaction and fellowship between Jews and Gentiles. Previously it had not been possible for the two groups to eat meals together due to the deep offence caused by, for instance, eating meat with the blood still included.

Jews believed that the blood was the life of an animal, and this belonged to God alone; if blood flowed away, life went too. So meat for the Jews was drained of blood in the slaughter process (kosher), and any other practice was unacceptable. The wisdom of James in demanding these simple conditions resulted in deep-seated barriers finally being broken down. In all other respects Gentiles kept their identity, were free from the Law and able to pursue their own customs and way of life. Faith in Christ was the only key needed for their salvation.

James had demonstrated the skills of a counsellor and mediator by making concessions to both parties without in any way compromising obedience to God's purposes.

4. Timothy

Paul's action in circumcising Timothy may look like double standards: since he had just won his point in the Jerusalem Council that circumcision was no longer essential for salvation, why did he now insist on immediate circumcision for Timothy?

The reason was probably that Timothy's mother was Jewish. The Jerusalem Council debate had been concerned not with Jews, for whom circumcision was the norm, but purely with regard to converts from the Gentiles. Paul probably felt that he would be laying himself open to further criticism from Jewish purists if his young missionary accomplice was found to be an uncircumcised Jew.

Paul's action can be seen as a further step forward in the breaking down of barriers for another reason: mixed marriages were not accepted by strict Jews. Feelings were so strong that the Jewish boy or girl would be considered dead, and on occasions a symbolic funeral would be conducted. By his recruitment of Timothy, Paul was demonstrating full acceptance of the son of such a marriage as a brother Jew.

5. Missing verse

What happened to Acts 15:34?

The Good News Bible (and other versions) recounts how Judas and Silas left the others to return to Jerusalem, while Paul and Barnabas continued to spend time in Antioch. Confusion then arises in v37-40 where it seems all are together. The Authorized Version contains a verse 34 which states: *'Notwithstanding it pleased Silas to abide there still.'* Scholars seem agreed that this was added later to answer the logistical problem, so most believe the verse should be left out.

DISCUSSION TOPICS

1. Sometimes we say, 'I'd go to him/her if I had a problem.' What personal qualities draw us to certain people? Does age play a part?

2. What sort of grouping (ages, numbers etc) is best to facilitate discussion and sharing in House Groups?

3. What events are good for encouraging people 'in the pews' to become more involved in church life and enrich their discipleship?

4. What value is there in continuing longstanding traditions of worship or church activities?

5. About what aspects of Christian life do we compromise when a) trying to accommodate the practices of the younger generation, b) mixing with non-Christians? Is this right?

6. Do you deal with tricky situations in person or by letter? Why?

7. What gifts can you offer to your church? Your community?

8. In what ways do you apply your reading of the Bible to daily life?

PRAYER

Praise the Lord.

I will extol the Lord with all my heart
in the council of the upright and in the assembly.

Great are the works of the Lord;
they are pondered by all who delight in them.
Glorious and majestic are his deeds,
and his righteousness endures for ever.
He has caused his wonders to be remembered;
the Lord is gracious and compassionate.
He provides food for those who fear him;
he remembers his covenant for ever . . .
. . . The works of his hands are faithful and just;
all his precepts are trustworthy.
They are steadfast for ever and ever,
done in faithfulness and uprightness.
He provided redemption for his people;
he ordained his covenant for ever –
holy and awesome is his name.

The fear of the Lord is the beginning of wisdom.

(from Psalm 111 N.I.V.)

Dear God, grant us the spirit of wisdom to follow you faithfully all the days
of our life.

AMEN

764 Christ from whom
784 Thy hand O God

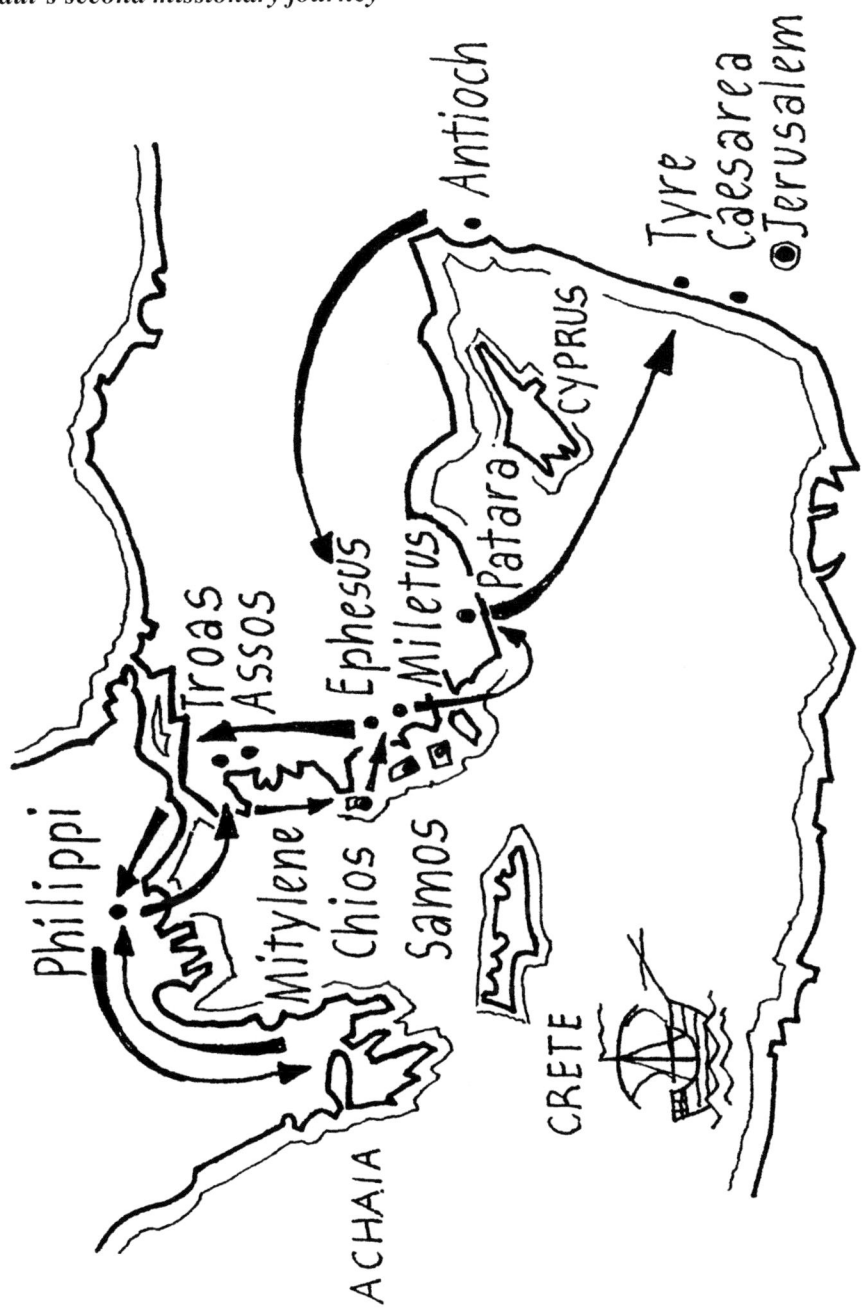

Paul's second missionary journey

LYDIA

Hello! Come in! Welcome to Philippi!

Now does anyone know what a murex is? . . . No? . . . Blank looks everywhere? I thought so! Well, I'll tell you in a moment, because I've a favourite thought which I like to share with everyone. First let me introduce myself.

People call me Lydia, and that's actually the name of the place I come from. Lydia's a region of Asia Minor and I was brought up there, in the town of Thyatira. It's a wonderful area – wealthy since the days of the unbelievably rich King Croesus who ruled in the sixth century BC. People say gold came pouring down the river in his time! It doesn't happen quite like that now, but towns like Thyatira are prosperous, cosmopolitan places where you gaze at stalls loaded with costly fabrics and exotic perfumes. If you've an eye for fashion – well, that's a 'must' on your tour schedule! I feel quite homesick, talking about it. What seemed unique to me was the impression of vibrant colour everywhere – Lydia seemed alive with it, or at least that's what sticks in my memory. Ever since childhood I've been surrounded by bright colours – for the obvious reason that the area is famous for textiles and carpets and all the dyeing and weaving that go with them. In a minute you'll see how the Lydia before you is a real daughter of this magical part of Asia Minor!

But, of course, you want to know how I come to be in Philippi, hundreds of miles from my home. That's where the murex I mentioned comes in. You see, I'm in business; I'm what people call a 'seller of purple'. So my work is dyeing fabric purple, then selling it. The special purple dye I use comes from the murex shellfish. It's a pathetic little creature till you open it and find the particular gland. Then out spurts this rich, exotic purple dye – a few drops enough to transform a length of fabric. From what I've said you'll realise it's very costly, as we have to find the shellfish, then go through the complicated procedure of releasing the dye. But d'you know, it's so highly prized that kings and wealthy rulers choose it above all else for their courtly robes, and I travel far and wide to meet their demands. So that's how I come to be in Philippi.

That's not the end of the murex story, but let me switch to my experiences here before you get fed up with me rabbiting on; you must hear the really important things which have transformed my life in the last few weeks.

45

They push thoughts of my homeland right into the background. This is what all my life has been leading to, I'm sure of that.

When I arrived here, I found a lovely place for myself and my household; I've no husband now, but at least I'm fortunate in having no money worries. The house is spacious and quite luxurious with rooms for all the family and to spare, and I can do my work in comfort. It takes up most of my time keeping the business ticking over, so I settled down quickly and hardly had time to miss my old home. Each week, though, I allowed myself just one luxury, because it was important to me, and that was my prayer time. You may think it odd as I'm not a Jewess – indeed, I wasn't really any religion – but I knew God was the force behind my life, somehow or other; it was to him I owed thanks for my many blessings. Yet I have to admit I longed for clearer guidance about how to show my gratitude. I couldn't make up my mind what God expected of me. Now it was just lucky for me that a small group of Jews – mostly women – used to meet each week for prayer, down by the river. So I joined them, and immediately treasured these little interludes of quiet and friendship. People welcomed and accepted me even though I didn't really belong.

One day a group of travellers from Jerusalem came to join us there by the river – Christian missionaries, they were . . . three men and a young lad. I took to them at once, there was just something about them. One of the men was a doctor and one a teacher, but it was the third – a tentmaker called Paul – who had me enthralled. He was – or I should say, he **is** – extraordinary: very small, bandy legs, really weird-looking, but something about him draws you like a magnet. I now recognise this as the power of the Holy Spirit, but, of course, I knew of no such thing then. As soon as they arrived, this Paul began talking to us, telling us all about the Christian God and how he loved and cared for us, and had done since the world began. This was such a new idea, a God who actually loved us – I'd always thought of a stern rabbi who made sure people did the right thing; if not, he'd be there with the punishments! And that wasn't all. Paul told us about God's son, Jesus, who, quite recently, lived and died on the earth so that he could save us from our sins. He even rose up from the dead, and, as he was leaving, promised us the Holy Spirit to live at the heart of our lives. What a story, isn't it? You know the details, so I don't need to say more. But it hit me that this was what I'd waited for. How could I belong to Paul's God, because that was definitely what I wanted?

Paul said all I must do was confess my sins and be baptised, so, believe it or not, friends, I rushed back to the house, grabbed my family, and asked the missionaries to baptise us then and there. And now I'm so happy, the colour of my life has changed from sand to vivid royal purple! D'you begin to see now where I started? With the little murex? You see, I thought of that shellfish which is hardly noticed until its old life dies; when its heart is opened up, brilliant purple dye spurts out and colours everything it touches. Surely that was the story of my baptism?

And now my empty rooms are all full. Paul and his friends have agreed to stay with me, and I pray that my home will become the meeting place for lots more Christians here in Philippi.

BIBLE PASSAGES

Acts 16:11-15

We left by ship from Troas and sailed straight across to Samothrace, and the next day to Neapolis. From there we went inland to Philippi, a city of the first district of Macedonia; it is also a Roman colony. We spent several days there. On the Sabbath we went out of the city to the river-side, where we thought there would be a place where Jews gathered for prayer. We sat down and talked to the women who gathered there. One of those who heard us was Lydia from Thyatira, who was a dealer in purple cloth. She was a woman who worshipped God, and the Lord opened her mind to pay attention to what Paul was saying. After she and the people of her house had been baptized, she invited us, "Come and stay in my house if you have decided that I am a true believer in the Lord." And she persuaded us to go.

Acts 16:40

Paul and Silas left the prison and went to Lydia's house. There they met the believers, spoke words of encouragement to them, and left.

ADDITIONAL BIBLE REFERENCE FOR PRIVATE STUDY

Philippians 1:1-11

BACKGROUND NOTES

1. Second missionary journey

Paul's second missionary journey again occupied him for about three years. The story extends from Acts 15:36 to 18:23. Paul set out from Antioch with Silas, and toured the churches of Syria and Cilicia; then he revisited other churches, delivering a letter from the Jerusalem leaders. A period of uncertainty followed, until a vision inspired him to resume his journey to places including Philippi, Thessalonica, Corinth, Ephesus and finally back to Antioch. The significance was that the gospel had now spread to Europe.

2. Lydia

Our 'seller of purple' originated from the city of Thyatira in the region of Lydia, and it is not certain whether her personal name was Lydia or whether she was simply being identified as 'the lady from Lydia'. It may even have been a trade name she had adopted. We can assume that she was a successful and wealthy business woman, as trading in dyed fabrics would have required substantial capital. This gives an interesting insight into the independent position which could be enjoyed by women in Asia Minor at that time. It is not known whether Lydia was unmarried or widowed, but one scholar observes that the Greek word 'oikos' used for her household in Acts 16:15 is sometimes used for a family with children and might indicate that she was a widow.

Regarding her beliefs, Lydia was probably a pagan who was drawn to the devout life of the Jews but was not a proselyte. Being a God-fearing lady she was quickly influenced by Paul's preaching, but Luke is careful to point out that it was the Lord who opened her heart to Christianity, not just the eloquence of Paul. This had the significance of being the first known conversion and baptism of a European household, and was seen as a step forward in mission of this second of Paul's journeys.

Another of Lydia's qualities was her gift for hospitality displayed when she quickly opened her home to Paul's party, and subsequently to the whole group of Philippian Christians. Paul would have appreciated this as he is known to have commended the gift of hospitality to all Christians. (*'Share your belongings with your needy fellow-Christians, and open your homes to strangers', Romans 12:13.*)

3. Thyatira

Thyatira, Lydia's home city, was situated near the Lycus River and was known for its profitable trade and industries. The chalky water was particularly good for fabric dyeing. Archaeologists have found inscriptions which show that, by Lydia's time, there were many trade guilds which included dyers, leatherworkers, coppersmiths, woolworkers and linenworkers. These guilds would have had a significant influence on all walks of life, and it is known that they also promoted idolatry and heavy drinking. Much of the labour of the industries was carried out by women in their homes. Archaeologists also found evidence of large numbers of vats, which bore witness to the flourishing dyeing trade.

Clothing must have been quite colourful, as many dyes had been developed: scarlet from madder root, crimson from insects, pink from pomegranates and yellow from crocus. It is possible that Lydia's 'purple' was the red from the madder root which was cheap and plentiful in Thyatira, and red was known to be a popular colour for Hebrew clothing, but Lydia's wealth leads many scholars to conclude that she traded in the more costly, rare and exotic dye from the murex shellfish. The dye was famous in the Near East, and much sought after. It was a rich purple colour and was extracted by a fairly complicated and skilful process from the gland of this small creature, native to the Mediterranean Sea.

Religion in Thyatira meant for most people the worship of pagan gods like Apollo, and these cults were energetically preserved into Roman times when the cult of emperor-worship would have been added. There was probably a small Jewish settlement in the city as well.

4. Philippi

Philippi was a city near the coast of Macedonia, which was given its name in the fourth century BC by Philip of Macedon. Towards the end of the first century BC it became a colony of Rome and so enjoyed the same rights and privileges as any town in Italy.

When Paul arrived there on his second missionary journey, the Jewish community must have been very small – and mainly female – as there was no synagogue in the city. According to Jewish Law there had to be ten men in regular attendance for a synagogue to be formed. Failing this, a place of prayer had to be established in the open air near to a river, where people could meet on the Sabbath for worship. The little group from Philippi was in the habit of meeting by the River Ganga, about a mile and a half from the city.

After her household had been baptised Lydia encouraged Paul and his party to stay at her house, and this Philippian home became the base for the first known European Christian community. One can tell from the warmth of Paul's letter to the Philippians, written from prison some years later, just how dearly he loved this congregation and appreciated what they had achieved together. (*'So then, my brothers, how dear you are to me and how I miss you! How happy you make me, and how proud I am of you!' Philippians 4:1*)

In the context of Lydia's purple-selling business it is interesting to note that archaeologists discovered in Philippi a Latin inscription with the word [PV]RPVRARI, which means 'to be made purple', and which testifies to the existence of purple-selling activities in the area at that time. Evidence also came to light of the presence of Christians in the city, in the form of two Latin crosses, but these came from a slightly later period.

DISCUSSION TOPICS

1. How important is prayer? Is it a regular part of your daily routine? Do you find meeting together for prayer helpful? Why, or – possibly – why not?

2. What are the most important things in your life? What adds colour, or do you feel colour is lacking?

3. How did you first become a Christian? Who or what had an influence on your decision?

4. Can you relate any experience where you felt God close to you?

5. What would you consider evidence of 'a true believer in the Lord' (Lydia's words)? How would Lydia's experience of God have differed before and after she met Paul?

6. Have you ever been really lonely? If so, what helped you through? In what ways are visitors or new people welcomed at your church?

7. Have you ever attended worship in a foreign country? What were your impressions?

8. Are the rights of women fully respected in our country now?

PRAYER

With Paul's words encouraging the church at Philippi (1:9-11):

I pray that your love will keep on growing more and more . . .

Dear Lord God, we are sorry that our love for you is often feeble and ineffective; sometimes it is hardly there at all when, in the bustle of life, we seem to forget you completely. We admire Lydia who went in search of you at the riverside, made you the centre of her life, and drew others in to share your love in fellowship. Reveal yourself to us, so that we too may draw close and catch sight of that perfect love which sent your Son into the world to live and die for us.

. . . with true knowledge and perfect judgement, so that you will be able to know what is best . . .

We ask you, Lord, to make us worthy disciples who seize every opportunity to learn more about you. You have given us a wonderful resource in the Bible; may we never tire of delving into its pages and learning more of your goodness to us. Help us to be attentive to preachers who throw light on your teaching and show us how to apply it to our lives. Above all, open our hearts to you in prayer, so that we are always at the ready, listening for your guidance.

. . . then you will be free from all impurity and blame on the Day of Christ.

Dear God, we are sorry for the ways in which we disappoint you. We are full of good intentions, but so often fail to carry them through. Forgive us, and strengthen us as we start afresh, secure in the knowledge that your hand is there to support us.

. . . Your lives will be filled with the truly good qualities which only Jesus Christ can produce . . .

We marvel, Lord God, at the enthusiasm of the early disciples which knew no bounds. Fill us with your Holy Spirit so that we too may be fired with the purpose of spreading your gospel. May the fruits of patience, love, peace and joy shine forth in our lives and lead others to your kingdom.

. . . for the glory and praise of God.

AMEN

JAILER

Cor, luv o' Reilly! You'll never believe this! Come on in, will you, and I'll tell all. Dunno whether I'm coming or going! Lucky I'm here at all really – could have been dead now, spiked on me own sword. I'm the jailer at Philippi prison, see, and we had this 'do' the other day. Folk said it was an earthquake, but it weren't as simple as that – no way! A blast from the Almighty, I calls it, or this 'ere Holy Spirit maybe. Fair knocked me sideways . . . ended up on me knees, shivering and shaking, I did! But the good bit was me and the missus and the family, we all got baptised, and now we're followers of the Christian God. Best thing we done in years! Funnily enough I said to the missus, 'We seems different people, you and me,' I sez. 'My thoughts exactly!' she sez, and only a week gone by! You dunno what you're missing sometimes till it hits you, and cor! did this hit us!

Ten days ago none of this had happened. Can hardly believe that meself! Just quietly going about my business, I was, doing me rounds, checking on the prisoners, cleaning up here and there, having a bit of lunch with the missus – this and that, nothing untoward. It's pretty quiet here in the provinces and, I have to say, it suits me nowadays – not getting any younger, as they say! I'm pretty careful in me job, I takes a pride in keeping things calm and orderly, like – guess it's the Roman in me. But we locks 'em all in tight here, specially the troublesome characters, so there ain't much can happen, to be honest. Leastways, that's what I figured till this how-d'ye-do put me straight!

I'd been hearing about a rumpus in the city square – word gets around quick here, see. Two foreigners had got theirselves into some sort of trouble and crowds was flocking to see the action, summat like that. Next I know, an order arrives that the two is on the way here – Paul and Silas their names – and I'm to lock 'em up real tight 'cos they've caused an uprising in the town. Bit surprised I was . . . I mean, seemed a bit over the top, two foreigners doin' all that, if you follow, but I don't ask no questions in this job. Just got things ready, like. I never did hear what it was all about till Paul himself tells me when it's all over. It appears a mad slave-girl was chasing him around, ravin' away, till he gets a bit fed up with it all – perhaps feels sorry for her, I dunno – so he decides to cure her with this power of his . . . or the power of this Holy Spirit, I should say. Well, it seems her folks had been piling up loads of cash from her capers and they wasn't best pleased with this new state of affairs; all the lovely money was going to dry up, see? So they trots off to the powers-that-be with some phoney story, and next thing Paul and his mate gets a beating in the square.

So, to continue me story – it was quite late when the foreigners was brought and a pretty sorry pair they looked – half dead from the lashing. 'They ain't going nowhere fast looking like that!' I sez to myself, but best do as I'm told, so I locks them away in the inside secure cell; even clapped their feet in the stocks for good measure, then off I goes to bed. Now listen carefully, this is where it all happens, the earthquake bit. It was near on midnight and we was fast asleep and snoring, me and the missus. BOOM! BOOM! SMASH! BANG! CRASH! SMASH! Dear o' Lor'! It's the end of the world, I thinks, as I leap up and grab my sword. Rush out. First thing I see, all the prison doors is wide, wide open – not broken off, you understand – wide open! Who could do that? And the chains? All them mighty chains is snapped, neat in bits, as though a giant had chopped them! It's the truth, I swear it.

'That's it!' I thought. 'Me number's up! All the prisoners gawn! I'll hang for this.' So I draw my sword, and as I go to throw meself on it – Luv-a-duck! What d'you think happens? I hear the voice of the foreigner, Paul, shouting out. 'Don't harm yourself! We're all here!' I couldn't even see him in the pitch black. Someone – dunno who – pushed a light into my hand and we rushed into the jail. Despite all the racket and shaking and cracking the cells was pretty normal – it was just the doors and chains. And there inside, cool as you please, was the prisoners! Well, I'm telling you, I'd had enough! Shaking like a leaf, I was, sweat pouring down me face, and I'm ashamed to admit it, I just fell down in a heap at their feet. 'Save me,' I begged. 'Show me what I've gotta do!' 'Cos I knew, see . . . I knew this was their God's work. So right there, in the middle of the night, Paul explained the lot. We – 'cos me family was all with us by now – we bathed their cuts and bruises with whatever we could get hold of, and Paul told us all about his kind and wonderful God.

Need I say more? You can see why we wanted such a God for ourselves. We said as much and Paul baptised us then and there – me and the missus and all the family. Then to prove we was genuine, we invited them over to my place and we finished up with a nice meal and a cosy chat. Stone the crows! Sounds like a kids' story, but that's how it was, folks!

Funny thing was, they wouldn't leave the jail, the two of them . . . stayed another couple of days! You'd think they'd scarper! But they was Roman citizens, see? Proud people, us Romans, and they wasn't going to leave without a proper apology from the magistrates. Oh yeah, they'd been told they could go, but they knowed their rights and they wasn't leaving till the officials had come cap-in-hand! Funny, really! Anyhow, they're off on their way now, and we're right choked to see them go. They've left us with this new life, though – that'll keep us going, me and the missus!

BIBLE PASSAGE

Acts 16:16-40

One day as we were going to the place of prayer, we were met by a slave-girl who had an evil spirit that enabled her to predict the future. She earned a lot of money for her owners by telling fortunes. She followed Paul and us, shouting, "These men are servants of the Most High God! They announce to you how you can be saved!" She did this for many days, until Paul became so upset that he turned round and said to the spirit, "In the name of Jesus Christ I order you to come out of her!" The spirit went out of her that very moment.

When her owners realized that their chance of making money was gone, they seized Paul and Silas and dragged them to the authorities in the public square. They brought them before the Roman officials and said, "These men are Jews, and they are causing trouble in our city. They are teaching customs that are against our law; we are Roman citizens, and we cannot accept these customs or practise them." And the crowd joined in the attack against Paul and Silas.

Then the officials tore the clothes off Paul and Silas and ordered them to be whipped. After a severe beating, they were thrown into jail, and the jailer was ordered to lock them up tight. Upon receiving this order, the jailer threw them into the inner cell and fastened their feet between heavy blocks of wood.

About midnight Paul and Silas were praying and singing hymns to God, and the other prisoners were listening to them. Suddenly there was a violent earthquake, which shook the prison to its foundations. At once all the doors opened, and the chains fell off all the prisoners. The jailer woke up, and when he saw the prison doors open, he thought that the prisoners had escaped; so he pulled out his sword and was about to kill himself. But Paul shouted at the top of his voice, "Don't harm yourself! We are all here!"

The jailer called for a light, rushed in, and fell trembling at the feet of Paul and Silas. Then he led them out and asked, "Sirs, what must I do to be saved?"

They answered, "Believe in the Lord Jesus, and you will be saved – you and your family." Then they preached the word of the Lord to him and to all the others in his house. At that very hour of the night the jailer took them and washed their wounds; and he and all his family were baptized at once. Then he took Paul and Silas up into his house and gave them some food to eat. He and his family were filled with joy, because they now believed in God.

The next morning the Roman authorities sent police officers with the order, "Let those men go."

So the jailer told Paul, "The officials have sent an order for you and Silas to be released. You may leave, then, and go in peace."

But Paul said to the police officers, "We were not found guilty of any crime, yet they whipped us in public – and we are Roman citizens! Then they threw us in prison. And now they want to send us away secretly. Not likely! The Roman officials themselves must come here and let us out."

The police officers reported these words to the Roman officials; and when they heard that Paul and Silas were Roman citizens, they were afraid. So they went and apologized to them; then they led them out of the prison and asked them to leave the city. Paul and Silas left the prison and went to Lydia's house. There they met the believers, spoke words of encouragement to them, and left.

ADDITIONAL BIBLE REFERENCE FOR PRIVATE STUDY

Galatians 3:26-29

BACKGROUND NOTES

1. The slave girl incident

The slave girl who upset Paul was said to have a spirit of divination, but the literal translation would have been 'a python spirit'. The reference is from classical mythology which told of a serpent that guarded the temple of Apollo and the Delphic oracle at Mount Parnassus. People believed Apollo was embodied in the snake, and used his power to endow his priestesses with the gift of clairvoyance. They saw ventriloquism also as the result of possession by this python spirit. It is not surprising, therefore, that the ancient world had a healthy respect for mad people, believing them to be somehow the embodiment of a god.

The title 'Most High God' was used both by Jews to refer to Yahweh and Greeks to Zeus, so the girl's recognition and acknowledgement of the Christians' power were screamed out in terms easily understood by all who heard her. Luke's language here is an echo of his report of Jesus' encounter with a demoniac who threw himself at his feet and shouted, *'Jesus, Son of the Most High God! What do you want of me?' (Luke 8:28).*

Although the girl's persistent shouting must have irritated Paul, the strong word used for his disquiet suggests something deeper than irritation, and probably refers to his grief at her disturbed condition. With typical compassion, he exorcises the demon and brings her peace of mind. The juxtaposition of this incident with the conversion of Lydia and the jailer invites us to conclude that she also became a believer.

2. Punishment

When the jailer describes Paul and Silas as 'a pretty sorry pair . . . half dead from the lashing', this would have been no exaggeration, as punishments at this time were brutally harsh. It is a tribute to their courage that they were able to lead prayers and sing hymns so soon after the experience. In a letter to the Corinthians Paul looks back on the horrors of the periods spent in prison during his journeys: '. . . *I have been in prison more times, I have been whipped much more, and I have been near death more often. Five times I was given the thirty-nine lashes by the Jews; three times I was whipped by the Romans' (2 Corinthians 11:23-25).*

So how was the law administered in the provinces? Most Roman colonies had two chief magistrates, often called *praetores,* and under them were two *lictorae* who carried bundles of birch rods with axes attached which symbolised their authority, and were used to carry out the beatings ordered by the magistrates. Prison officers were frequently ex-army personnel who could be relied on to obey any further instructions with military precision and toughness. If they allowed a prisoner to escape, they were liable according to Roman law to the same penalty as that due to be paid by the escapee.

The charge against Paul and Silas was of promoting an alien religion and thereby disturbing the peace. Although the grudge of the slave girl's masters was really financial, they cleverly manipulated it to stir up the latent anti-Semitic feeling which was rife throughout the Roman empire. So successful were they in rousing the crowds against the Christians that reasoned debate about the issues was clearly impossible, and the magistrates settled for a quick beating and night in jail, no doubt hoping this would teach the troublemakers the required lesson. It is likely that they were also sympathetic towards the slave girl's owners. Thus although Paul and Silas, as Roman citizens, should have been exempt from such treatment, mob rule seems to have won the day.

It is interesting that there is no word of the part played here by Luke and Timothy, but it is probable that they had less of a Jewish appearance and that the magistrates contented themselves with the two leaders.

3. Imprisonment and release

Jewish punishments for crime in the years BC had tended not to favour imprisonment, quick retribution and correction being more to their liking. Their magistrates would no doubt have viewed our twenty-first-century penal system as counter-productive. The aims of punishment for them would be repayment to victims, quick punishment for offenders, and likely execution for any who posed a threat to society. Surrounding countries had probably made regular use of prisons earlier than Israel, and the jail at Philippi was, of course, Roman.

Life in prison in the first century AD would certainly not have been a picnic, wherever you were. Buildings were usually crude, sometimes little more than a hole in the ground, and cells were dark and often damp. Those described as 'inner' or 'secure' might even be underground dungeons. Prisoners could be chained or beaten or confined in wooden stocks, all three of which were suffered by Paul and Silas on this occasion. They were probably underfed, and forced to perform hard labour.

To prevent escape, the doors of the Philippi jail would have been secured by heavy wooden bars that fitted into two slots, and a similar device may also have been used to hold the chains and the stocks. Earthquakes were not uncommon in the area, and so this natural phenomenon in itself would have been no surprise to the jailer. It is conceivable that the violent shaking could have thrown out the retaining bars, making escape possible without any miraculous intervention, but this is not how Luke saw the events: he placed the incident straight after the slave girl's recognition of Paul and Silas as servants of an all-powerful God, and made careful mention of the fact that they were praying and singing hymns just before the earthquake happened, thus signalling this as God vindicating his two faithful servants and paving the way for the conversion of the jailer.

The next morning the magistrates sent the lictors to the jail with the order to release Paul and Silas, but there is no mention of the earthquake.

Presumably the authorities had not heard of its effect on the prison but were intending to free the prisoners after one night anyway. However, Paul refused to let them overlook the rights of Roman citizens to travel anywhere in the empire under the protection of Rome and untouched by local legislation. By making the claim 'Civis Romanus sum' ('I am a Roman citizen'), an individual asserted his immunity to punishment.

Since there were heavy penalties for violation of this privilege, the Philippian magistrates wasted no time in making amends.

4. Three converts at Philippi

Luke writes in Acts 16 of the conversion of three very different people, – different in race, different in social class, different in personal qualities – but all welcomed into the fellowship of Jesus Christ at the new church in Philippi.

Lydia was a wealthy, capable, influential lady from Asia Minor; the slave girl was Greek, had no rights or possessions and would have been judged the lowest of the low on the social scale; the jailer – probably a Roman ex-army man – would be considered respectable middle class, and somewhere mid-way between the two. There were reasons why all three would have been despised by extremists of the Jewish church (as Gentiles, slave etc.), but now all were free to be followers of the Christian God – another leap forward for the Early Church.

DISCUSSION TOPICS

1. In what ways might you see a change in people who have become Christians?

2. Why do you think this experience caused the jailer to believe in God?

3. Do you believe in miracles? How far do we need them to believe?

4. Do you think prison sentences are effective? Should they be longer/shorter? What punishments do you think are effective for children who do wrong?

5. Do you worry about injustice? If so, what can Christians do about it?

6.   Why do you think church membership seems to appeal more to middle-class people?

7.   How do you think people outside the church view our God? Punitive? Remote?

8.   What sort of things cause argument and division in churches? How important are they?

PRAYER

Make me a captive, Lord,
And then I shall be free;
Force me to render up my sword,
And I shall conqueror be.
I sink in life's alarms
When by myself I stand;
Imprison me within thine arms,
And strong shall be my hand.

My power is faint and low
Till I have learned to serve;
It wants the needed fire to glow,
It wants the breeze to nerve;
It cannot freely move,
Till thou hast wrought its chain;
Enslave it with thy matchless love,
And deathless it shall reign.

My will is not my own
Till thou hast made it thine;
If it would reach a monarch's throne
It must its crown resign;
It only stands unbent,
Amid the clashing strife,
When on thy bosom it has lent
And found in thee its life.

George Matheson (1842-1906)

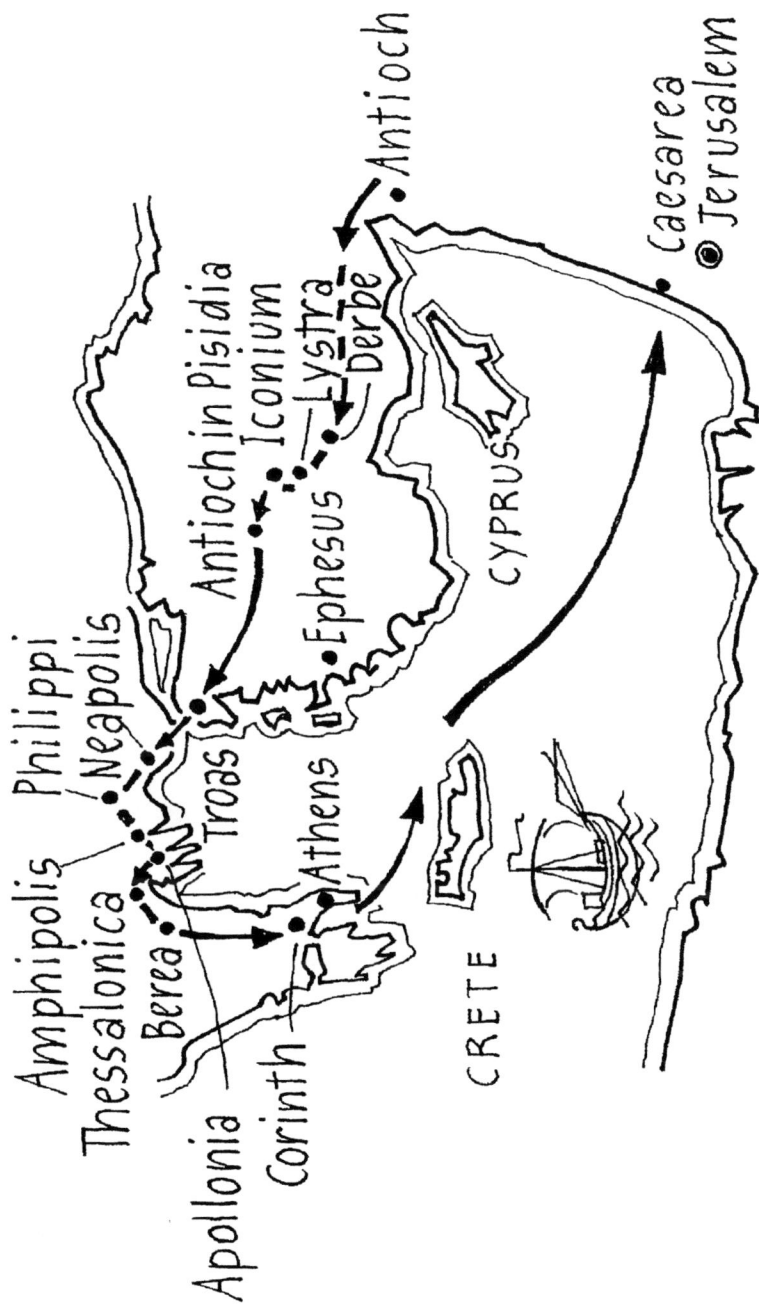

Paul's third missionary journey

AQUILA AND PRISCILLA

Priscilla: Hi, everyone! Welcome to our shop! I'm Prisca – Paul calls me that, but most people call me Priscilla – and this is my husband, Aquila. I'm really glad you've caught up with us here because our mission has just had a terrific boost and I'm dying to tell someone about it: we've been entertaining the distinguished Alexandrian preacher, Apollos – d'you know him? – in fact, we had to teach him all that Jesus did after . . .

Aquila: *(interrupting)* Aren't you starting rather late in our story, my dear?

Priscilla: Sorry, have I said something wrong?

Aquila: No problem there, my love. I just thought our visitors need to know a bit about us first. Otherwise we could sound a little presumptuous, don't you think?

Priscilla: Could we? How terrible! Of course, you're right as usual. I'm just so thrilled with what's happening here in Ephesus, I get carried away!

Aquila: That's as good an introduction to my wife as you'll get, friends! Yes, she's a great enthusiast, and I wouldn't wish it otherwise. There's always some new Christian to tell you about, or some lost missionary who needs a meal, and it all brings such blessing to our home.

Priscilla: It's what I always wanted when we got married: I wanted our home to be a place for Christians to meet and have fellowship together. Then when Paul landed up with us, it was like the icing on the cake! . . . But I'll do as you say, dear husband, and start at the beginning.

Aquila is a Jew from Asia Minor, and we got married in Rome where my family lived. Aquila had moved there from Pontus on the coast of the Black Sea. He's a tentmaker, and we set up our first business there in Rome. It was such a thrill – people seemed to arrive on our doorstep from far and wide. We were so proud of it, and I suppose we expected to stay there years. Most important of all, Rome was where we first heard the wonderful news about Jesus Christ, and we both decided without hesitation to follow his way. Since then our single aim has been to tell as many people as possible about him.

Unfortunately there was a lot of squabbling and skirmishing among the Jews in Rome at the time, with all the new ideas, and it became so bad that the emperor suddenly pronounced that all Jews were to leave the city.

Aquila: What a shock it was, particularly for you, my dear.

Priscilla: I was devastated! Couldn't believe they'd throw me out of my own city. But I'd always had a sneaking wish to travel like you, so we talked about it and plumped for Corinth. The Lord must have something in mind for us, we said – let's go for it!

Aquila: I'd heard Corinth was good for trade; also there were people of all nationalities, including a large Jewish community, so we should be welcome there.

Priscilla: We quickly found a place and set up our second business. Again it took off really well and our home was full of new Christian friends. Then Paul turned up on the doorstep! I'll never forget that first impression: he was so small and sick-looking – he seemed at his last gasp, and really down, and yet he drew you to him like a magnet. He was like a wounded lion.

Aquila: He'd had a terrible time in Athens, and he was still suffering from that dreadful flogging in Philippi.

Priscilla: D'you remember how thrilled he was to find we were tentmakers like himself? We all had so much in common! Paul needed to work, so he decided to stay at our place and join the business. It was great while it lasted: he preached on the Sabbath and worked with us the other days. Then one day friends of his turned up with some money from the Philippi church, and he was able to move out and concentrate on preaching full time.

When the church was safely established in Corinth, and our business there had been up and running for about three years, we got itchy feet! Paul had to go to Syria, so we paid for the trip and joined him. We stopped off here in Ephesus, and it looked so good we decided to stay. People wanted Paul to stay as well but he had things to see to in Jerusalem. He promised to try and come back later, but we haven't seen him again yet.

Aquila: Perhaps you could tell them your exciting news now?

Priscilla: Apollos, you mean? I'd nearly forgotten! I was thinking how much we've missed Paul since he went away. But yes, Apollos! Jesus would probably tell me off for being so excited about him – all people are equally important, I know, and we certainly meet lots here. But Apollos is rather special! He's a distinguished orator with such a gift for interesting people and holding their attention – absolutely wonderful for our missionary work. And I've never come across anyone so knowledgeable about the Scriptures!

We first heard him at the synagogue here; he was speaking about Jesus and you'd have said he was on fire with the Holy Spirit – you could have heard a pin drop. But d'you know, the strange thing was that his preaching didn't seem up to date: baptism for him seemed to be just the baptism of John.

Aquila: We couldn't believe it when he seemed so wise and learned.

Priscilla: So what we did – and I must be careful because this is where Aquila says I sound presumptuous – what we did was to invite him home so we could fill in the missing bits . . . to help him, if you see what I mean. He was so gracious – not at all miffed that we were correcting him – just grateful for the information and enthusiastic about how it would strengthen his case. What a brilliant mind he has! He plans to go to Corinth so we're writing to tell the church people there. Lucky lot! I wish Paul was here to talk to him.

Aquila: You're always wishing Paul was here, my dear. It's a good thing I understand you so well!

Priscilla: I don't mind admitting Paul is my greatest inspiration since we embarked on Christ's mission. I just love him.

Aquila: I believe you'd die for him.

Priscilla: Yes, I would, we both would, but it wouldn't be for him as a person, it would be for Jesus Christ.

Aquila: The way things are, it may yet come to that. We've already had some hairy moments. Let's pray that the Holy Spirit will give us the strength to face whatever lies ahead.

Priscilla: Amen to that! Now let's all have something to eat. I'm starving!

BIBLE PASSAGES

Acts 18:1-5

After this, Paul left Athens and went on to Corinth. There he met a Jew named Aquila, born in Pontus, who had recently come from Italy with his wife Priscilla, for the Emperor Claudius had ordered all the Jews to leave Rome. Paul went to see them, and stayed and worked with them, because he earned his living by making tents, just as they did. He held discussions in the synagogue every Sabbath, trying to convince both Jews and Greeks.

When Silas and Timothy arrived from Macedonia, Paul gave his whole time to preaching the message, testifying to the Jews that Jesus is the Messiah.

Acts 18:18-28

Paul stayed on with the believers in Corinth for many days, then left them and sailed off with Priscilla and Aquila for Syria. Before sailing from Cenchreae he had his head shaved because of a vow he had taken. They arrived in Ephesus, where Paul left Priscilla and Aquila. He went into the synagogue and held discussions with the Jews. The people asked him to stay longer, but he would not consent. Instead, he told them as he left, "If it is the will of God, I will come back to you." And so he sailed from Ephesus.

When he arrived at Caesarea, he went to Jerusalem and greeted the church, and then went to Antioch. After spending some time there, he left and went through the region of Galatia and Phrygia, strengthening all the believers.

At that time a Jew named Apollos, who had been born in Alexandria, came to Ephesus. He was an eloquent speaker and had a thorough knowledge of the Scriptures. He had been instructed in the Way of the Lord, and with great enthusiasm he proclaimed and taught correctly the facts about Jesus. However, he knew only the baptism of John. He began to speak boldly in the synagogue. When Priscilla and Aquila heard him, they took him home with them and explained to him more correctly the Way of God. Apollos then decided to go to Achaia, so the believers in Ephesus helped him by writing to the believers in Achaia, urging them to welcome him. When he arrived, he was a great help to those who through God's grace had become believers. For with his strong arguments he defeated the Jews in public debates by proving from the Scriptures that Jesus is the Messiah.

ADDITIONAL BIBLE REFERENCES FOR PRIVATE STUDY

✔ *Romans 16:3-10*

1 Corinthians 16:19

2 Timothy 4:19

BACKGROUND NOTES

1. Aquila and Priscilla

Aquila and Priscilla are mentioned six times in the New Testament and on four occasions Priscilla's name is written first, twice by Paul and twice by Luke. This suggests she may have played a more important or lively role in the Early Church activities than her husband, although both were wholeheartedly committed to its mission. Priscilla was probably more cultured, with a background that was both Roman and Hellenistic; some scholars believe she wrote the Letter to the Hebrews, although others – including Martin Luther – suggest Apollos. Prisca is the name of a well-known Roman family, so she may have been wealthy and able to provide backing for the tentmaking business. Aquila was a Jew from Pontus in Asia Minor, possibly a slave or freedman.

The couple, who were much-travelled, seem to have moved back to Rome after the death of the Emperor Claudius – information which can be deduced from Paul's greeting to them in his Letter to the Romans *(Romans 16:3)*. They may have retained their business in Ephesus and alternated between the two, which would account for Paul greeting them in his Letter to Timothy, who was still resident there *(2 Timothy 4:19)*.

Aquila and Priscilla were close friends of Paul, and tireless workers for the Christian Church. He refers to them affectionately as his *'fellow-workers in the service of Christ Jesus'*. There is no talk of them being his converts, so they had probably become Christians before leaving Rome. Their loyalty to Paul was such that they were prepared to risk their lives for him *(Romans 16:4)*. It is not known how or when this occurred, but scholars suggest it may have been in the rioting caused by silversmiths in Ephesus after Paul's return to that city.

2. Third missionary journey

Paul's third missionary journey begins at Acts 18:23, where Luke describes him leaving Antioch for a tour of Galatia, Phrygia and beyond. He revisited and encouraged some of the churches, and Timothy was again one of his companions. This journey included the best part of three years in Ephesus and ended with sad farewells to the elders of the Ephesian church; Paul had warned them of troubles awaiting him in Jerusalem.

3. Tentmaking

Most English versions of the Bible give the trade of Aquila, Priscilla and Paul as tentmakers because the literal translation of the Greek word means this. However it may have had a wider connotation such as 'leatherworker', as tents in the ancient world were usually made of leather. A further possibility is 'clothworker', as Paul's native region of Cilicia was famous for *cilicium,* a coarse goats' hair fabric used for clothing and curtains as well as tents.

By New Testament times most people were living in houses, and tents were used mainly by shepherds and nomads, but in the ancient times of the patriarchs most common dwellings were tents. They were made by stretching cloth – usually animal skins – over poles which were set in the ground, and more elaborate versions would have curtains to act as room-separators, and carpets or mats to cover the floor. There might even be holes in the centre for kindling fires.

Because the concept of tent-dwelling was rooted so deeply in the Jewish heritage, it has been used widely in literary imagery. To most Jews it suggested protection, comfort and even hope. Perhaps the most interesting example is John 1:14: *'The Word became a human being and . . . lived among us.'* Here the word 'lived' is a translation of the Greek *skenos* which means a tent, so John could conceivably have pictured Jesus 'pitching his tent' among us, a very homely and reassuring concept.

4. House church

Aquila and Priscilla kept open house for Christians, and in his letters to both Corinthians and Romans Paul refers to their home being a church. They played host to the new Christians of Ephesus for four or five years. In one of Paul's letters they join him in sending greetings from this Ephesus church to their old one in Corinth *(1 Corinthians 16:19).*

The synagogue was the place where Jewish people worshipped, and if they became new converts to Christianity, many still continued to worship there. For several decades many Jewish Christians maintained this tradition. But for some, the house church became the answer. The early Christians possessed no church buildings, and there is no record of any being provided until the third century. The natural development was for a Christian family possessing a room big enough to offer its home as a meeting place for worship, prayer and fellowship. Services were based on the Jewish pattern, with psalms and hymns being sung, prayers said, and passages read from

Scripture. To these were added stories of Jesus, letters from church leaders, and teaching about how it all fulfilled the Old Testament writings. They were also taught how the gospel should be applied to daily life. Fellowship meals would be shared in memory of the Lord's Supper. At the end of prayers, people would greet each other warmly with the kiss of peace – a tradition which features still in many contemporary liturgies in the form of the passing of the Peace, and which was encouraged by Paul in Romans 16:16: *'Greet one another with a brotherly kiss'*.

We have already seen how Lydia's home became a centre for the Christian church at Philippi, and similarly John Mark's mother, Mary, kept open house for believers in Jerusalem. For Jews the concept of household had always been sacred, so this extension of its function to include a place for worship was an obvious step for the new Christians. The Christian communities generally had no formal leadership, but trusted the Holy Spirit to bind them all together – Jews and Gentiles, rich and poor, cultured and artisan, and people of every nation. Such a mix around the dining table would have been unthinkable when Paul's mission work first began.

5. Corinth

The original city of Corinth was destroyed in 146BC in a Greek revolt against the Roman Empire, but it was rebuilt in the time of Julius Caesar as a Roman colony, and in 27BC became the capital of the province of Achaia. Its population in New Testament times was probably over two hundred thousand, comprising a mixture of many nationalities and a substantial number of Jews. Due to its situation on an isthmus by a fearsome waterway, trade routes all converged there and its prosperity was assured. It was one of the most prosperous and influential cities of the period.

This had a darker side, however: Corinth was notorious for debauchery and immorality of every kind. Even before the time of Paul, the phrase 'to live like a Corinthian' was slang for a drunken or immoral lifestyle.

The city was the centre for the worship of Aphrodite, goddess of love, and her great temple towered above the city. It boasted a thousand prostitutes who masqueraded as its priestesses, and their activities were legendary. In addition, there were temples and shrines to numerous other pagan gods. Paul must have felt daunted when he arrived there exhausted from the setbacks of Philippi and other places along the way, and found such an unlikely setting for a Christian church. Despite the gloomy prospect, he preached and taught there for a year and a half and, to quote William Barclay, *some of the mightiest triumphs of Christianity were won*.

6. Apollos

Apollos was a learned Jew from Alexandria, who arrived in Ephesus in the year 53AD, while Paul was away in Antioch. He was an eloquent and spirited speaker with an impressive knowledge of the Scriptures, who captivated audiences and inspired them with his colourful teaching. He had received instruction somewhere about Jesus, and knew the gospel up to a point, but there were deficiencies in his understanding of the Christian message: he knew baptism in the name of John, but not of Jesus.

When Aquila and Priscilla heard him in the synagogue, they immediately recognised his gift for preaching, but were concerned that his message was incomplete. They invited him home and explained the vital news of all that God had done through the death and resurrection of Jesus, and how his Holy Spirit had been sent to comfort and empower the believers. When the time came for Apollos to leave Ephesus and begin a new teaching ministry in Corinth, the church there quickly responded to his powerful and persuasive expositions of the Christian message. He used his encyclopedic knowledge of Scripture to prove that Jesus was the predicted Messiah.

He became a prominent church leader there and, according to the fourth-century scholar, Jerome, became the first bishop of Corinth. He was highly respected by Paul, despite the difference in their style of preaching.

DISCUSSION TOPICS

1. How can we use our homes for Christian service?

2. What things make you really joyful a) at home b) at work c) in church?

3. What particular skills or abilities can you offer a) to the work of the church b) to the community?

4. Does an open welcome to everyone cause any problems for the church? If so, how can you resolve the issues?

5. What makes a good preacher? What makes a good member of the congregation?

6. How do you account for the rapid growth of the House and Community Churches? Why do you think people sometimes choose their informality instead of the more structured leadership of the established churches?

7. Are you good at accepting criticism? If not, how can you improve?

8. In what practical ways can we live out our faith outside the church?

PRAYER

Breathe on me, Breath of God;
Fill me with life anew,
That I may love what thou dost love,
And do what thou wouldst do.

Breathe on me, Breath of God,
Until my heart is pure,
Until with thee I will one will,
To do and to endure.

Breathe on me, breath of God,
Till I am wholly thine,
Until this earthly part of me
Glows with thy fire divine.

Breathe on me, Breath of God;
So shall I never die,
But live with thee the perfect life
Of thine eternity.

Edwin Hatch (1835-89)

DEMETRIUS

Hey, you! Come over and listen to me for a bit. Those fancy talkers have been working on you, I've seen them, and I've just about had enough! My name's Demetrius and I've a business to run here, with scores of workers dependent on me – it's no laughing matter! You hear our side of the story. It's pie in the sky, what they're telling you. Get in the real world, I say! We're craftsmen, all this crowd – silversmiths, to be exact – and we're the pillars of this community. We keep our fine city in business, but if this interfering bunch get their way, there won't be any business left in Ephesus. Get the picture? How would you like it if all your industry was messed up by some crank? Cool cheek they've got, dropping in from the other side of nowhere and turning our lives upside down. What do they know about Ephesus? They've not been here five minutes! Ours is a great city, the treasure house of Asia, and we're proud of it – it's not some ramshackle shanty town in need of a makeover.

Let me tell you about it, and maybe you'll see things differently, right? First of all, Ephesus has always been prosperous and people live a good life here. We've about half a million inhabitants, and by and large they've no cause for complaint – nice houses, streets paved with marble, great shopping, magnificent buildings, baths, libraries . . . this huge theatre where we gather for meetings; it's a good life – or it has been – and that's the way we mean to keep it. So you watch out, eh? We know what makes a place tick, and we don't need interfering foreigners telling us how to do our job. It's all about trade. Without that you're as good as dead. You've seen Corinth, right? Well, that's a great commercial city, and so is Ephesus here. But to have trade you need traders, right, and that's where we come in. I'll come back to that in a minute.

The second point is, we're very religious here; we take spiritual matters seriously and temple worship is the main ... **wait a minute! I'm beginning to get angry, sir**! I'm not blind, you know! I saw that smirk on your face! I will repeat what I said and I speak in deadly earnest: **we...are...a...very...religious...city...** got it? And that's precisely why we don't need all these fine ideas the Christians are hawking around. I'd go so far as to say it's religion that has made Ephesus so prosperous. Why do you think the Romans call us temple-keepers, eh? You must have seen our temple – you can't miss it. It was built four hundred or so years ago, and it's one of the seven wonders of the world. In case you don't know, it's four times as big as the Parthenon in Athens, and contains more paintings

73

and sculptures than you could wonder at in a day. Pilgrims flock to it from far and wide, to say their prayers among its glittering marble pillars – a hundred and twenty-seven, it has, each one the respectful gift of a king. And who do they come to worship? Is it some piffling demigod who guards your bedside or smiles on your dining table? No sir! We're talking about the most noble Artemis, great mother goddess of fertility, honoured and idolised for centuries in cities throughout the world. Great will be her vengeance on those who scorn her! She has dominated for so long that no one can tell of her coming – we believe she dropped out of the heavens. Her grand altar was carved by Praxiteles, greatest of all Greek sculptors, and she is served in the temple by more priests and attendants than you could count, and thousands of the purest slave-girls await her bidding.

Ah! Now you are impressed, eh? Gone pretty quiet, haven't you? Beginning to see we Ephesians aren't the bunch of brainless idiots you took us for, is that it? Good! We're getting somewhere! Now you want to know how I and my silversmiths feature in this grand temple scene, right? I'll tell you.

As I mentioned, pilgrims come here from all over the world to worship the goddess. Naturally they need images to focus their thoughts. My silversmiths – and all the others in the union here – provide this service to the best of their ability with exquisitely fashioned silver keepsakes. The tourists immerse themselves in the emotional rituals of the temple, then as they leave they are comforted by the little souvenirs clutched to their bosoms. **Who dares to deny them this blessing?** What cruel trick is in the mind of this Paul and his Christians? What gain is he after? Eh? Is he happy with the hurt he causes? Answer me that! To say nothing of the damage to our city, to the temple and – most of all – our noble goddess herself! This upstart has lectured people all over Asia about our goddess being rubbish, so what happens? They don't come here any more. 'No need to bother about pilgrimages,' they say. 'It's all a waste of time. Let's go to the races!' they say. Does that seem good to you, neglecting their worship? And for what, I ask? The Christian has them all fighting and falling over each other in confusion while our time-honoured goddess is neglected and our temple falls into disrepair. 'They're not confused at all,' I heard someone say. Oh yes, they are! I know, I've seen it! I've seen crowds arguing with priests, and priests punishing preachers. Wherever they go they start trouble, you take my word! The people are confused all right!

I haven't even mentioned the hardship side of it for me and my employees. We have to work for a living, you know. No work, no cash! It's as simple as that, so we roll up our sleeves and get carving as fast as we can, to keep our families. You ask my mates. Hopping mad, they are, I can tell you – hundreds of them, and they're out for blood! 'Your rewards are in heaven!' chants this charlatan. What's that supposed to mean for a man with a wife and six kids? Give us something we can get our hands on, that's all we want. And we've got it right here – at least we did have till all this started. But we've got our act together and we'll soon send them packing, believe you me! The whole union is behind me and we'll show them which god has the power in this city, you see if we don't! **Praise to our goddess! Great is Artemis of the Ephesians!**

BIBLE PASSAGES

Acts 19:23-41

It was at this time that there was serious trouble in Ephesus because of the Way of the Lord. A certain silversmith named Demetrius made silver models of the temple of the goddess Artemis, and his business brought a great deal of profit to the workers. So he called them all together with others whose work was like theirs and said to them, "Men, you know that our prosperity comes from this work. Now, you can see and hear for yourselves what this fellow Paul is doing. He says that gods made by human hands are not gods at all, and he has succeeded in convincing many people, both here in Ephesus and in nearly the whole province of Asia. There is the danger, then, that this business of ours will get a bad name. Not only that, but there is also the danger that the temple of the great goddess Artemis will come to mean nothing and that her greatness will be destroyed – the goddess worshipped by everyone in Asia and in all the world!"

As the crowd heard these words, they became furious and started shouting, "Great is Artemis of Ephesus!" The uproar spread throughout the whole city. The mob seized Gaius and Aristarchus, two Macedonians who were travelling with Paul, and rushed with them to the theatre. Paul himself wanted to go before the crowd, but the believers would not let him. Some of the provincial authorities, who were his friends, also sent him a message begging him not to show himself in the theatre. Meanwhile the whole meeting was in an uproar: some people were shouting one thing, others were shouting something else, because most of them did not even know why they had come together. Some of the people concluded that Alexander was responsible, since the Jews made him go up to the front. Then Alexander motioned with his hand for the people to be silent, and he tried to make a speech of defence. But when they recognized that he was a Jew,

75

they all shouted together the same thing for two hours: "Great is Artemis of Ephesus!"

At last the town clerk was able to calm the crowd. "Fellow-Ephesians!" he said. "Everyone knows that the city of Ephesus is the keeper of the temple of the great Artemis and of the sacred stone that fell down from heaven. Nobody can deny these things. So then, you must calm down and not do anything reckless. You have brought these men here even though they have not robbed temples or said evil things about our goddess. If Demetrius and his workers have an accusation against anyone, we have the authorities and the regular days for court; charges can be made there. But if there is something more that you want, it will have to be settled in a legal meeting of citizens. For after what has happened today, there is the danger that we will be accused of a riot. There is no excuse for all this uproar, and we would not be able to give a good reason for it." After saying this he dismissed the meeting.

Isaiah 40:18-25

To whom can God be compared?
How can you describe what he is like?
He is not like an idol that workmen make,
that metalworkers cover with gold
and set in a base of silver.
The man who cannot afford silver or gold
chooses wood that will not rot.
He finds a skilful craftsman
to make an image that won't fall down.

Do you not know?
Were you not told long ago?
Have you not heard how the world began?
It was made by the one who sits on his throne
above the earth and beyond the sky;
the people below look as tiny as ants.
He stretched out the sky like a curtain,
like a tent in which to live.
He brings down powerful rulers
and reduces them to nothing.
They are like young plants,
just set out and barely rooted.
When the Lord sends a wind,
they dry up and blow away like straw.

To whom can the holy God be compared?
Is there anyone else like him?

ADDITIONAL BIBLE REFERENCES FOR PRIVATE STUDY

Acts 19:1-20

Ephesians 4:1-16

BACKGROUND NOTES

1. Ephesus

Ephesus was founded around the eleventh century BC by colonists from Athens who saw it as a valuable link between the Eastern and Western worlds, and a gateway to the riches of Asia. Due to its strategic position at the end of a great trade route and at the mouth of the River Cayster, it became renowned as a commercial and cultural centre, but by Paul's time things had started to go wrong: its fine harbour was beginning to silt up, causing problems for the trade which was its great source of prosperity. The silting was blamed on excessive use of the fertile hinterland for intensive grazing, forestry activity and charcoal burning, all of which conspired to send the topsoil into the river where it was washed down to choke up the estuary. Numerous efforts were made over the centuries to relieve this problem, but the silting continued, such that today the old harbour of Ephesus is seven miles from the sea, behind a swamp.

The resultant reduction in trade suffered by the Ephesians of Paul's time forced them to depend more on their other claim to fame – religion. The city was an important religious centre from the Roman point of view, as the cult of emperor-worship flourished there, and Ephesus boasted as many as three temples dedicated to this end. However, it was as a worship centre for the great pagan goddess Artemis that it acted as a magnet for thousands of pilgrims and tourists from far and wide, thus providing opportunities for trade of a different sort. Ancient writers seemed to judge that, as a place of pagan pilgrimage, it even outstripped the famous gardens of Babylon and the Colossus of Rhodes.

The vast temple of Artemis was the jewel in its crown, but in keeping with its recent reputation as a city of enormous prosperity, Ephesus boasted an array of beautiful buildings. There was a stadium which hosted the Pan-Ionian Games watched by the whole country, and there was a giant theatre

– used also as a meeting place – which seated more than twenty-five thousand people and is still in a good state of preservation. The splendid main street, which ran straight from the theatre to the harbour, was about thirty-five feet wide with a monumental gateway at each end and colonnades on either side. To both north and south of this street were fine buildings to cater lavishly for the physical and intellectual needs of the inhabitants.

With so much at stake, it was clearly not going to welcome any new philosophy which threatened this way of life!

2. Artemis

Artemis was the pagan goddess worshipped most widely throughout the Greek world, and corresponded to the Roman goddess, Diana. However, the goddess of the Ephesians and most cities of Asia had little in common – except the name – with this fair virgin huntress of classical mythology: she was not a virgin but a voluptuous Asian mother-figure; not a moon-goddess but a goddess of fertility in humans, animals and vegetation. Her worship was dark, mysterious and oriental, a far cry from the open-air image of the Roman goddess, Diana. The image of her, positioned by the grand altar in the temple, was certainly no beauty, in fact it was probably not the image of a goddess at all. It was a colossal dark lump with a suggestion of 'many-breasted' about its crude contours. People believed it to be a meteorite which had fallen from the sky. (Meteorites in other cities, such as Troy, had become sacred cult objects in just this way.) However unattractive she might appear, the goddess clearly had a huge following.

The fabulous temple to Artemis in Ephesus, which was situated one and a half miles from the city, was built in the fourth century BC on the site of a previous sanctuary. It was the size of St. Paul's Cathedral in London, with a hundred and twenty-seven Ionic pillars sixty feet high supporting a white marble roof. Thousands of pilgrims flocked to it and, as a pilgrimage centre, it was as famous as Jerusalem. The Romans were sufficiently impressed with the city's religious provision to accord it the title of temple-keeper. This was usually bestowed on cities maintaining temples for emperor-worship, but an inscription and coins have been found indicating that Ephesus was also honoured as guardian of the temple of Artemis.

The temple was also a sort of international bank where merchants, kings and even cities could deposit money in the safe keeping of the goddess. The Roman historian, Pliny, writes that the temple was destroyed seven times and was finally ruined in 263AD by the Goths. Some of its pillars were used to build the church of S. Sophia in Constantinople.

Other 'religious' boosts to the Ephesian economy in Paul's time consisted of income from the provision of food and accommodation for the pilgrims, and the trade in deity memorabilia. Regarding the latter, Ephesus had long been a centre of pagan superstition and, as well as the Artemis keepsakes, there was a profitable business in charms and spells known as the Ephesian Letters, which were guaranteed to solve virtually any problem under the sun (a far cry from the requirements of the Trade Descriptions Act!).

To the early Christian missionaries this deep-seated cult of Artemis presented some of their strongest opposition.

3. Demetrius

Although a 'baddie' in the annals of the Early Church, Demetrius was probably not a particularly evil man on the sliding scale of human behaviour. His motives were almost certainly mercenary, and devotion to Artemis played second fiddle to profits from his silverware, but many contemporary employers would feel sympathy for the threat Paul presented to his employees, the declining profits of his business and his very position as boss.

We know that he was a very successful businessman, that he had a large workforce of his own, and that he had authority with the other traders in the city's union of silversmiths. He had the natural ability of a working man of the people to inflame them corporately, with threats to their security and orchestrated slogan-shouting. Paul's condemnation of man-made gods throughout the area was being seen to be very effective, and their industry was clearly on the line. The workers were enraged.

So what was it that they made? The silver keepsakes were unlikely to have been models of the goddess, in view of her strange appearance and the lack of any surviving relics; they were generally thought to be silver models of the first primitive sanctuary which was replaced by the great temple. The surroundings of the temple would have been alive with displays of these souvenirs and most visitors would have succumbed to the tempting of the traders.

4. The Holy Spirit's achievements in Ephesus

With a long tradition of pagan idolatry, superstition and practice of magic, the population of Ephesus was rough ground for the Christian missionaries, and yet many converts were made, and some magic practices were publicly renounced. Paul's mission lasted about three years and he left soon after the incident with the silversmiths. By then the church of Ephesus was firmly established, and Paul could write to it years later from his prison cell.

It is interesting to note where in Ephesus Paul's preaching took place. As was his custom, he began in the Jewish synagogue, but after problems there he moved to more neutral ground in the form of a lecture hall – the hall of Tyrannus. He continued in this location for two years, presumably using it when it was free from its customary usage. Despite the difficulties, Paul received encouragement in several ways: Luke records miracles which took place such as the cure of sick people by handkerchiefs which had touched Paul *(Acts 19:11-12),* and there was encouragement from the Roman authorities who, in the form of the town clerk, dismissed opposition to his missionary activities. Most important of all, many new converts joined the Christian Church.

DISCUSSION TOPICS

1. What do you think 'religious' meant to the Ephesians before they were converted to Christianity? What does it suggest to people in our society nowadays?

2. Do our denominational differences turn people against Christianity? Are such differences always wrong?

3. Do you have any sympathy for the arguments put by Demetrius in the script? Are there modern parallels or lessons to be learnt? Are trade unions a positive or negative force?

4. How can we bring Christian witness into our day's work? What might we do to ensure our rights, and those of others, in the workplace?

5. Can Christian beliefs conflict with your employment? If so, in what ways, and how do you handle it?

6. How should Christians in our multi-faith society interpret Christ's instruction to spread the gospel?

7. What exactly do we mean by religious tolerance, and how far should it go?

8. Demetrius in his script says that what the disciples are saying is 'pie in the sky'. What arguments do you use to counter this?

PRAYER

Dear God, we marvel at the amazing complexity of your creation which results in each one of us being unique. We look and sound different, have different gifts and abilities, think different thoughts,
and make different choices.
But in making wrong choices for our lives,
we often sabotage your grand design:
we please ourselves, and forget other people;
we cling to our point of view, ignoring the reason of others;
or sometimes we are easily persuaded when your way is to stand firm;
we see the good in ourselves, but the bad in others;
we use gifts and abilities to better our lot,
sometimes at the expense of others.

Forgive us, Lord, and teach us how to follow you more closely. May the perfect example of Jesus always be alive in our hearts, and may the Holy Spirit fire us to serve you faithfully and enthusiastically
to the end of our days.
For Jesus' sake

AMEN

PAUL

So now it's my turn! I thought I'd catch it sooner or later! Welcome, my brothers and sisters in Christ! Meet Saul – or rather Paul – of Tarsus! I'm not sure what you'll make of me – I'm a complex bundle of trouble, or so my good friend Prisca tells me. I've had my highs and lows, and this spell in jail is not what I'd have chosen, but the Holy Spirit is still here, pulling me through it all. He never gives up, and that's the immense, immeasurable blessing of my life. If I were to tell you what he's done for me, we'd be here till kingdom come, so I'll try to highlight how God's hand has directed me from day to day.

First, let me ask how things are with you, down there in the twenty-first century? What splendid opportunities everywhere for the followers of Jesus! The gospel has been with you from the cradle; the cross adorns churches throughout the earth. There is not just one generation of witnesses now who can call your name, but over eighty! So how goes it? Are you on the Lord's side? Is the Spirit working through you? If not, you're living as slaves – slaves to money, slaves to ambition, slaves to desire, slaves to fashion – you're empty vessels like the young Saul of Tarsus. But Jesus called me, and with him in my heart I was set free. In Christ I became a new man. So come on, then, his grace is there for everyone, and with his grace you are free!

Yes, as a young man I thought I knew God. I was born in Tarsus in a good home with all that I could wish for; I was brought up a strict Pharisee, obedient to all that Jewish tradition demanded. I knelt at the feet of the great scholar Gamaliel, and was thrilled by the history of our race and every word of his teaching. I absorbed all I could by listening, reading and learning, and I earned my living with a trade. I was your ideal student. I dedicated myself to God, and saw a fulfilling life of service stretching ahead of me as a rabbi in the great Temple at Jerusalem. So when a new faction threatened, in the form of these Followers of the Way, what would you expect? Of course, I drew my sword and went on the attack.

But, friends, I didn't then have the marks of Jesus branded on my body; I didn't have Jesus in my heart; I was not living for his cause. I'm the most worthless apostle; perhaps I shouldn't be called an apostle at all, after persecuting God's church the way I did. But he was waiting for me. When the day came and he took hold of me, there was no doubt in my mind: everything up to that moment was rubbish; everything could be dumped.

The knowledge of Christ Jesus my Lord was all that mattered, and all I wanted now was to share his suffering and become like him. Here's what happened.

We were in full swing with the Jerusalem persecutions when the High Priest agreed I should go to Damascus to root out any Followers there and bring them back for trial. As I approached the city it was midday and the sun was at its hottest; that's not usually a problem, but suddenly the glare turned into an incredible searing light that flashed and threw me on the ground. I'm not one for fairy stories, so you'll believe me when I say that, as I grovelled on the ground, a voice spoke to me, saying calmly and unmistakably, 'Saul! Why are you persecuting me?' When I stammered who was it, he said, 'Jesus of Nazareth!' and he ordered me to go to Damascus. There I'd be told what God had in mind for me. I was incapable – so blinded by the light that my fellow-travellers had to drag me up and lead me by the hand. They'd seen the light but not heard any voice. They got me to Damascus, and I was wondering what to do next when a visitor called – Ananias – a wonderful godly man whose healing touch restored my sight. He set me on track for my new life with the Holy Spirit. He even called me 'brother'! Imagine that from a man who surely must have wished me dead. I experienced God's grace and immediately felt invigorated to get out and tell everyone about Jesus. I wanted every bone in my body to ache with the efforts of this one great purpose. Make no mistake! It wasn't easy. Who'd want to listen to a monster like me? But when the hostility of my fellow Jews became intolerable, the Lord directed me to travel far away and take the news to the Gentiles. I've been travelling ever since.

What exciting times! The Spirit has led me far and wide across land and sea, through sunshine and storms, through barren desert and fertile farmland, through sleepy villages and sophisticated societies, to races who understand my languages and others who don't. On every journey people have listened to the good news about Christ Jesus, and vast numbers have come to know God's grace. One or two special places leap to mind: the church at Philippi – so dear to my heart – sprang from a prayer group which met by the riverside; Lydia, a visitor from Thyatira, was moved by the Spirit and asked me to baptise her. Then she opened her home as a meeting place for the believers. In Corinth I was led to the house of Aquila and Prisca, who share my trade of tentmaking; they're such great workers for the Lord, and they too open their house for prayer meetings. They've been amazing friends and even risked their lives for me on one occasion. In Ephesus there was such exciting work to be done that three whole years flew past. When the Spirit called me to move on, the church was well established and energetic in its mission. I had a final meeting with the leaders where we knelt together for prayer. The sense of God's presence and the warmth of our fellowship were intense. Luke and I had to tear ourselves away and many tears were shed.

My travels have also brought suffering: I've been whipped, I've suffered illness, I've been stoned, I've been shipwrecked, I've been in danger from Gentiles and – worst of all – from fellow-Jews. This last is a gaping wound for me, as I've struggled all my life to be loyal to my roots. But traditionalists accuse me of turning people against the Law of Moses, and their plotting has resulted in my spending these valuable years in prison. But I'm happy with this setback suffered for Christ's sake, since he's assured me that his power is strongest when I am weak.

So, dear brothers and sisters, I guess that brings me up to date. And what of the future – the future for me, and the future for you in the twenty-first century? I'm dead certain we must leave the past and set our sights on what lies ahead. Run like mad for the finishing line and claim the prize that's there for all of us – the prize of life for ever in God's kingdom.

May the grace of the Lord Jesus go with you!

BIBLE PASSAGES

Acts 20:24

But I reckon my own life to be worth nothing to me; I only want to complete my mission and finish the work that the Lord Jesus gave me to do, which is to declare the Good News about the grace of God.

Acts 21:17-28

When we arrived in Jerusalem, the believers welcomed us warmly. The next day Paul went with us to see James; and all the church elders were present. Paul greeted them and gave a complete report of everything that God had done among the Gentiles through his work. After hearing him, they all praised God. Then they said, "Brother Paul, you can see how many thousands of Jews have become believers, and how devoted they all are to the Law. They have been told that you have been teaching all the Jews who live in Gentile countries to abandon the Law of Moses, telling them not to circumcise their children or follow the Jewish customs. They are sure to hear that you have arrived. What should be done, then? This is what we want you to do. There are four men here who have taken a vow. Go along with them and join them in the ceremony of purification and pay their expenses; then they will be able to shave their heads. In this way everyone will know that there is no truth in any of the things that they have been told about you, but that you yourself live in accordance with the Law of Moses. But as for the Gentiles who have become believers, we have sent them a letter telling them we decided that they must not eat any food that has been offered to idols, or any blood, or any animal that has been strangled, and that they must keep themselves from sexual immorality."

So Paul took the men and the next day performed the ceremony of purification with them. Then he went into the Temple and gave notice of how many days it would be until the end of the period of purification, when a sacrifice would be offered for each one of them.

But just when the seven days were about to come to an end, some Jews from the province of Asia saw Paul in the Temple. They stirred up the whole crowd and seized Paul. "Men of Israel!" they shouted. "Help! This is the man who goes everywhere teaching everyone against the people of Israel, the Law of Moses, and this Temple. And now he has even brought some Gentiles into the Temple and defiled this holy place!"

Acts 22:6-21

"As I was travelling and coming near Damascus, about midday a bright light from the sky flashed suddenly round me. I fell to the ground and heard a voice saying to me, 'Saul, Saul! Why do you persecute me?' 'Who are you, Lord?' I asked. 'I am Jesus of Nazareth, whom you persecute,' he said to me. The men with me saw the light, but did not hear the voice of the one who was speaking to me. I asked, 'What shall I do, Lord?' and the Lord said to me, 'Get up and go into Damascus, and there you will be told everything that God has determined for you to do.' I was blind because of the bright light, and so my companions took me by the hand and led me into Damascus.

"In that city was a man named Ananias, a religious man who obeyed our Law and was highly respected by all the Jews living there. He came to me, stood by me, and said, 'Brother Saul, see again!' At that very moment I saw again and looked at him. He said, 'The God of our ancestors has chosen you to know his will, to see his righteous Servant, and to hear him speaking with his own voice. For you will be a witness for him to tell everyone what you have seen and heard. And now, why wait any longer? Get up and be baptized and have your sins washed away by praying to him.'

"I went back to Jerusalem, and while I was praying in the Temple, I had a vision, in which I saw the Lord, as he said to me, 'Hurry and leave Jerusalem quickly, because the people here will not accept your witness about me.' 'Lord,' I answered, 'they know very well that I went to the synagogues and arrested and beat those who believe in you. And when your witness Stephen was put to death, I myself was there, approving of his murder and taking care of the cloaks of his murderers.' 'Go,' the Lord said to me, 'for I will send you far away to the Gentiles.'"

1 Corinthians 15:8-12

Last of all he appeared also to me – even though I am like someone whose birth was abnormal. For I am the least of all the apostles – I do not even deserve to be called an apostle, because I persecuted God's church. But by God's grace I am what I am, and the grace that he gave me was not without effect. On the contrary I have worked harder than any of the other apostles, although it was not really my own doing, but God's grace working with me. So then, whether it came from me or from them, this is what we all preach, and this is what you believe.

Now, since our message is that Christ has been raised from death, how can some of you say that the dead will not be raised to life?

Philippians 3:5-11

I was circumcised when I was a week old. I am an Israelite by birth, of the tribe of Benjamin, a pure-blooded Hebrew. As far as keeping the Jewish Law is concerned, I was a Pharisee, and I was so zealous that I persecuted the church. As far as a person can be righteous by obeying the commands of the Law, I was without fault. But all those things that I might count as profit I now reckon as loss for Christ's sake. Not only those things; I reckon everything as complete loss for the sake of what is so much more valuable, the knowledge of Christ Jesus my Lord. For his sake I have thrown everything away; I consider it all as mere refuse, so that I may gain Christ and be completely united with him. I no longer have a righteousness of my own, the kind that is gained by obeying the Law. I now have the righteousness that is given through faith in Christ, the righteousness that comes from God and is based on faith. All I want is to know Christ and to experience the power of his resurrection, to share in his sufferings and become like him in his death, in the hope that I myself will be raised from death to life.

ADDITIONAL BIBLE REFERENCES FOR PRIVATE STUDY

Acts 9:1-19

Philippians 3:12-14

2 Corinthians 11:22-31

2 Corinthians 12:7-10

BACKGROUND NOTES

Paul

Paul is a giant of the Christian faith – arguably the chief missionary of early Christianity – whose life and letters have influenced the world throughout the past two thousand years, so it is impossible to do justice to him in a large volume, let alone a single chapter. These notes can only offer a simple introduction, which may tempt the reader to delve more deeply into Paul's own writings or the many scholarly works written about him. The legacy of his letters contained in the Bible is considerable, giving insight as it does into both the achievements and the problems of the churches he founded, and his own attitudes and emotions as he thinks about them. What better source, then, for the monologue at the start of this chapter? This small attempt to bring him to life has been compiled largely from his own words, used, as far as one can judge, in the contexts he intended. Nevertheless the limitations of trying to turn such a complex character from the distant past into flesh and blood are obvious, and the script should be seen as no more than a starting point for research or discussion.

The following notes are by way of pointers to more detailed study.

1. Name

Paul is first mentioned in the Book of Acts by his Hebrew name, Saul. As a Jew he would be proud to bear the name of Israel's first king. However, it is likely that, as a citizen of Rome, he possessed from birth the additional name of Paul. Luke links the two names in the account of Saul's clash with Elymas on the island of Cyprus (*'Then Saul – also known as Paul' Acts 13:9)*, and thereafter the writer uses the name Paul exclusively. It no doubt seemed appropriate to use the Graeco-Roman name as Paul's mission became more involved with the Gentiles.

2. Appearance and character

From all accounts Paul's bodily size and appearance were not his most valuable assets! Few facts are available, but the second-century writer, Onesiphoros, describes him as follows in the apocryphal *'Acts of Paul and Thecla'*:-

'a man rather small in size, bald-headed, bow-legged, with meeting eyebrows, a large red and somewhat hooked nose, strongly built, full of grace; for at times he looked like a man, and at times he had the face of an angel.'

Early frescoes of Paul lend weight to this description. We can assume that, at the time of his missionary journeys, he would also have looked tanned, weather-beaten and scarred from his flogging and other harsh treatment.

What Paul lacked in visual attractiveness, he more than compensated for by his personality. He was a complex, dynamic character and a born leader who was not afraid to wield his authority. Some writers have portrayed him as a harsh and difficult man but they do him an injustice, as there is just as much evidence of love, gentleness and compassion in his relationships. He clearly had great charisma and could quickly draw huge crowds and influence them with his message. These words are all used regularly in descriptions of Paul: sensitive, generous, warm-hearted, tough, courageous, hot-tempered, demanding, a strong capacity for friendship, richly gifted, a born leader, a ceaseless worker and a human tornado! The phrase he himself would probably choose would be 'in Christ'. From the moment of his conversion Paul saw himself as a new man, totally dedicated to the service of his Lord. (*'When anyone is joined to Christ, he is a new being'* *2 Corinthians 5:17*) He would take no credit for achievements, but saw them always as the work of the Holy Spirit.

3. Background and early life

There were three strands to Paul's background: he was a citizen of Rome; he was steeped in the language and culture of Greece; and he was first and foremost a Jew (*'a pure-blooded Hebrew' Philippians 3:5*).

He was born in the city of Tarsus – a provincial capital of the Roman Empire situated in what is now Turkey – in about 10AD, and he inherited Roman citizenship from his father. Throughout his life he showed pride in both his birthplace (*'born in Tarsus in Cilicia, a citizen of an important city' Acts 21:39*) and his citizenship. The latter gave him certain rights, privileges and exemptions, which he valued and was quick to use to his advantage.

Tarsus was at that time an important university city with about five hundred thousand inhabitants, and was a meeting-place of cultures – East and West, Greek and Oriental. The cultural institutions were mainly Greek, and so Paul grew up familiar with Greek culture, knowledgeable in Greek literature and philosophy, and speaking the colloquial Greek of the region.

Above all, he saw himself as a Jew (*'I myself am an Israelite, a descendant of Abraham, a member of the tribe of Benjamin' Romans 11:1*). His love for the Jewish race and heritage permeates all that we read by him or about him. Paul was a Pharisee, and the son of a devout Pharisee, who had his son educated in the synagogue school with the strict upbringing that would prepare him for service as a rabbi. As was customary with Pharisees, he also learnt a trade to earn his keep, the craft of tentmaking or leatherwork. Towards the end of his teens he went to Jerusalem to study theology under Gamaliel, a distinguished member of the Sanhedrin. He would probably have been living with his sister at that time. Ten years later he was an acknowledged expert on Judaism and defender of its tradition, and it was at about this time that trouble started with the Greek-speaking section of the Christian community in Jerusalem. Stephen, one of their chief spokesmen, was persecuted following a blistering attack on certain events in Jewish history. Paul, who, with his strict orthodox beliefs, had already developed a hatred of the Christians, was seen to approve the stoning to death that followed.

4. Conversion on the road to Damascus

Paul's own account of this momentous, life-changing experience is given in Acts 22 quoted above, and Luke's earlier version is found in Acts 9:1-19. Nothing can be added to these dramatic accounts.

There has been much speculation by scholars about whether the Damascus conversion was indeed a 'lightning strike' or rather the climax of a process. The latter might have started with the stoning of Stephen: Paul had witnessed the cruel scene from a vantage point close enough to observe the radiance on the martyr's face as he committed himself to Jesus, and to hear Stephen's request for the persecutors to be forgiven. Could the conscientious and sensitive sides of the Pharisee fail to be moved? Might seeds of doubt germinate there? The fact that his behaviour became yet more ruthless from that moment could even be an attempt to stifle feelings of guilt. What would his thoughts have been as he plodded towards Damascus in the heat of the day?

Whatever conflicts may have occupied his mind, there can be no doubt as to the sudden, dramatic and decisive conquest and conversion brought about that day by the Holy Spirit. Paul spoke of it in some detail on numerous occasions.

One is put in mind of the sudden experiences of two other great Christian preachers, Augustine of Hippo, who 'saw the light' as he read verses from Romans 13 in a garden in Milan, and John Wesley in the eighteenth century, who felt his heart 'strangely warmed' at a prayer meeting in Aldersgate Street, London. As theologian Frances Young has commented, such a conversion can best be described as '*the end-product of a long search*' where '*the past was not so much rejected as taken up in a new way*'.

5. Paul's message

Before his conversion Paul's beliefs hinged on the sharp distinction between the Jews, who were the chosen race, and the Gentiles, who could only find salvation if they accepted circumcision and embraced the Jewish Law. Conversion knocked this distinction on the head by instilling in Paul the certainty that salvation came through the grace of God in Jesus Christ, and it was freely available for everyone. The news of this was to be conveyed to the ends of the earth. 'Grace' became one of Paul's watchwords and it appears eighty-six times in his writings.

His teaching was different from that of other apostles in that he had never known Jesus in the flesh, and so he rarely mentions his life and teachings. Christ's death and resurrection are, however, all-important. He saw in the cross the means of redemption and – significantly for his mission – the reconciliation of all people. The grace and mercy of God for everyone is the main thrust of his message, no doubt inspired by the experience of his own conversion: the risen Jesus had come to him despite the violence Paul had been directing at his followers.

Paul also taught justification by faith, rather than works.

His mission began with a baptism of fire and a test of both courage and conviction, as he launched his preaching in the streets and synagogues of Damascus, the very city that knew him as a tyrant and awaited the horrors he had come to inflict. Was this new approach some sort of trap? Paul's preaching was so powerful and his proofs about Jesus so convincing that crowds listened to him, but a body of resentment remained. A group made plans to kill him and he was forced to escape to Jerusalem.

It is no surprise that there also his preaching met with suspicion and opposition, such that Paul returned to his native town of Tarsus. Barnabas summoned him from there to assist with the Christians in Antioch, and it was some time before the Holy Spirit, in about 47AD, sent the two men to take the gospel to Gentiles overseas. This was the start of Paul's missionary journeys and the beginning of his role as leader of this outreach.

Within about ten years he had established the Church in Galatia, Macedonia, Achaia and Asia, all provinces of the empire where it had not existed hitherto. With each community Paul's missionary policy was the same: believers would be taught the basic doctrines of the Christian faith by Paul and by apostles; elders from within the group would be appointed as a sort of pastoral team; the community would be committed to the Lord, and then Paul would go on his way, leaving them to manage their own affairs *(Acts 14:23)*. Periodically he would return to check up on them, or write letters (particularly if he was restricted by imprisonment) to encourage and make suggestions.

Whilst crowds flocked to hear his message, the conflict with traditional Jews smouldered on, and he endured much hardship each time trouble flared. Finally, on a trip to Jerusalem for Pentecost, Paul was seized by a Jewish mob and forced to spend several years in custody in Caesarea.

6. Imprisonment

The rift between strict traditional Jews and those sympathetic to Paul's campaign of welcome for all comers to Christ, haunted Paul throughout his ministry, and was behind several periods he spent in prison. It hinged on the necessity of circumcision and strict adherence to the Jewish laws for all men who asked to become Christian. Paul insisted this meant trusting external issues rather than giving one's **heart** to God as he demanded. James, leader of the Jerusalem church, attempted to establish a new compromise code of conduct for the acceptance of Gentiles *(Acts 15),* but throughout his journeys Paul encountered violent opposition from reactionary Jews in local synagogues.

One such incident which resulted in captivity for Paul occurred in 57AD when he was arrested in Jerusalem and transported to the fortress of Caesarea for his own safety; it is this scenario which forms the backcloth for the imaginary monologue at the start of this chapter: church leaders in Jerusalem had accepted and generally welcomed Paul's news of widespread Gentile conversions, and recognised them as the hand of God at work, but trouble broke out when word was passed around that he was stirring Jews to neglect the Law. Although these accusations were unfounded and Paul made strenuous efforts to prove his loyalty to the tradition, he was arrested and a long spell of imprisonment followed. The governor, Felix, delayed judgement for reasons of his own convenience and it was only when his successor, Festus, took office that the deadlock was broken, and Paul was conveyed to Rome, at his own request, to be tried by the emperor according to his right as a Roman citizen.

7. Later life

On arrival in Rome Paul lived under house arrest but with access to friends and visitors. Many of his letters date from this period, including Colossians, Ephesians and Philemon. This last contains hints that he was expecting to be released soon and hoped to revisit Asia, but there are no facts recorded as to whether this took place. Scholars see clues in the letters to Timothy and Titus – assuming these **are** the work of Paul's hand – that he did return to Asia, Achaia and Macedonia, and also that he judged the end of his time to be drawing near. Eusebius, the fourth-century Bishop of Caesarea, records that Paul was taken back to Rome and killed during Nero's persecutions in 67AD. Other ancient writers claim that he was beheaded on the left bank of the River Tiber about three miles from Rome, at a place which became known as the Three Fountains. His body was believed to have been buried at the site of the present Basilica of St. Paul Outside the Walls, which is dedicated to his memory.

DISCUSSION TOPICS

1. What do **you** think was in Paul's mind when he watched the stoning of Stephen?

2. What views might Paul express about how we witness for Christ today? wimps - what witness?

3. What opportunities do you find for talking about your faith outside church or house group? - not many - more opportunities to show faith practically

4. What difficulties face Christianity in our society? Are they the same for all denominations of the church? *depends on type of witness* *Some denoms. more acceptable than others*

5. What tips for your Christian journey have you learnt from a study of Paul? *own life worth nothing* *never turn away from the vision* *Be who we are*

6. Do we pay too much attention to a) dogma or b) the business of the church, and not enough to the moving of the Holy Spirit? If so, how should we set things right? *Do we need ministers?*

7. To what extent should Christians involve themselves in politics? When is it right for Christian leaders to speak out publicly on such issues?

8. How important is Paul's role in the development of Christianity?

PRAYER

> *Lord God,*
> *I am no longer my own but yours.*
> *Your will, not mine, be done in all things,*
> *wherever you may place me,*
> *in all that I do*
> *and in all that I may endure;*
> *when there is work for me*
> *and when there is none;*
> *when I am troubled*
> *and when I am at peace.*
> *Your will be done*
> *when I am valued*
> *and when I am disregarded;*
> *when I find fulfilment*
> *and when it is lacking;*
> *when I have all things,*
> *and when I have nothing.*
> *I willingly offer*
> *all I have and am*
> *to serve you,*
> *as and where you choose.*

Glorious and blessèd God,
Father, Son and Holy Spirit,
you are mine and I am yours.
May it be so for ever.
Let this covenant now made on earth
be fulfilled in heaven.

AMEN

(Methodist Covenant Prayer)

381
42

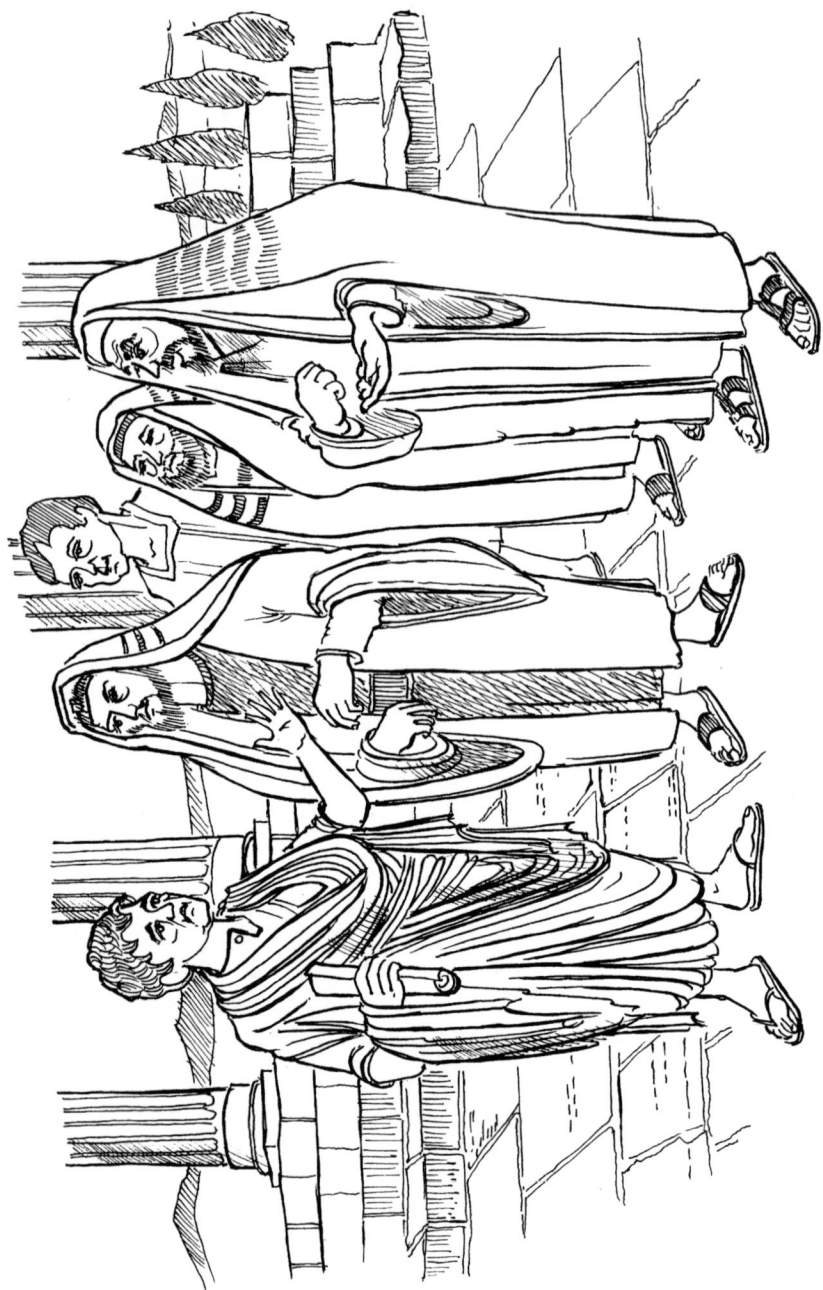

PORCIUS FESTUS

Good morning! Come in! I'm Porcius Festus, Roman procurator of Judaea, as I imagine you're aware. I must apologise if I appear inhospitable, but I can only spare a couple of minutes – I have a tight schedule. In any case, what I have to tell you will not take long since I've been here less than four weeks. I've worked flat out since I took up office here in Caesarea, familiarising myself with the Judaean scene. I'm currently trying to grasp the various ideologies that motivate all the sections of the population; easy, you may think, and an obvious requirement of my position, but you won't realise just how complex the issues are. But I get to grips with things quickly, and everything will soon be shipshape, never fear!

As you probably know, my appointment occurred as a result of the last procurator being withdrawn by the emperor, Nero, so I had precious little time to research things and prepare myself in the usual way. It was a case of 'Climb on, and **then** grab the reins!' or that's how I interpreted it. Anyway, it seems that my predecessor had thrown all pride in Rome to the winds, and allowed things to spiral out of control; he handled troublemakers either with bestial brutality or complete disinterest – locking some away for years and acting as though the problem had gone away. As far as I can see, he had no ability to confront issues and find solutions. Consequently Judaea was in a parlous state when I took over, with lawlessness everywhere and factions brandishing weapons at each other. It didn't take a statesman to deduce that the province was heading pell-mell for destruction, despite the safeguards of Roman administration. My problem was that I'd never had direct experience of Jewish affairs, and they're unbelievably complicated. I pride myself on being a fair-minded individual, and insist on absorbing all the background before I make judgements – over-cautious, if you like, but that's the Roman in me.

So much for me, but if I'm not mistaken, your interest is more with the Pharisee, Paul of Tarsus, who has been the first thorn in my side here. Is that it? Well, I have to tell you the matter is no longer in my hands as – at the fellow's own request – I've referred it to the emperor, and Paul is on the high seas, *en route* for Rome, even as we speak. However, I'll tell you briefly the events to date.

What you have to understand is that this man is in head-on collision with his own associates, the Jewish leaders. It took a while for me to grasp that, but then I took it as a warning sign: anyone who campaigns vigorously –

even ruthlessly – for an organisation, then suddenly switches to the opposition and slaves equally passionately for them has questions to answer. It smacks of instability of some kind, and I'm wary of that. Again my Roman training – we're mistrustful of extremist or fanatical behaviour in any guise. Paul's case wasn't helped for me by the irrational event which prompted his change of heart, nor by the supernatural elements in his Messiah story. That left me speechless. I'll run through what happened.

I was told the minute I got here about this chap being held in the prison – in fact he'd already been there two years, but that's no surprise if you remember my predecessor's habits. I was in Jerusalem three days after taking up office, and the Jewish leaders collared me and demanded that Paul be brought there for trial. The charges were serious, but I wasn't agreeing just like that. I spent a great deal of time with them, as it was important for those leaders to see me as an upholder of justice. The safest tactic was to stick rigidly to the Roman procedure for complaints such as this, so I told them to come back with me and confront Paul with their accusations in my presence. This they did, but their accusations had changed from those they'd mentioned to me, and seemed trivial and irrelevant. Paul insisted he was innocent on all counts, which left me with a dilemma: I wanted to satisfy the leaders, but I'm still not entirely sure of my ground on Jewish affairs, so I suggested to Paul that he stand trial in Jerusalem. Whereupon he upstaged me by using his privilege to appeal to the emperor. You could say that was the end of it for me, because, of course, I agreed. Then an unexpected opportunity cropped up to test the wisdom of my decision. Before we could arrange Paul's escort to Rome, I received a courtesy visit from King Agrippa and Queen Bernice. The king is steeped in Jewish lore, and I couldn't have wished for a better counsellor. Like me he was intrigued by the affair, and demanded to meet Paul. I arranged this for the very next day, and it was an extraordinary experience. You see, in my official capacity I refuse to be swayed by emotion – it so often clouds good judgement – but for the first time I let out an involuntary shout of disbelief at what I was hearing. I'm embarrassed to admit it, but that's how it was.

I realised from the start that Paul is a shrewd, highly-educated man and a convincing speaker. He started by telling us what I already knew – his life as a Pharisee in Jerusalem, and the so-called life-changing experience on the way to Damascus, which I guess was some sort of fit; but then he came out with this story about a Messiah who has to suffer and then rise from the dead, and that was too much! The story just didn't fit the man! That's when I shouted, 'You're crazy!' The king didn't seem surprised, and took it all in his stride. It didn't change the outcome anyway: we all agreed that no offence had been committed and, as the king said, if Paul hadn't appealed to the emperor, he probably could have gone home.

So now he's on his way to Rome. I'm pleased I was able to deal with the matter so quickly. In quiet moments, though, I do wonder that a mature, intelligent man of the world can languish in jail for two years, then emerge recounting exactly the same story with just as much energy and conviction. Could he be right and all of us wrong? But that's absurd!

Anyhow, I must be off – I'm late! He's quite a distraction, that Paul and his Jesus talk. I suppose the only thing I have in common with Procurator Felix is that neither of us knew what to make of him! Goodbye!

BIBLE PASSAGES

Acts 24:27 and Acts 25:1-12

After two years had passed, Porcius Festus succeeded Felix as governor. Felix wanted to gain favour with the Jews so he left Paul in prison.

Three days after Festus arrived in the province, he went from Caesarea to Jerusalem, where the chief priests and the Jewish leaders brought their charges against Paul. They begged Festus to do them the favour of bringing Paul to Jerusalem, for they had made a plot to kill him on the way. Festus answered, "Paul is being kept a prisoner in Caesarea, and I myself will be going back there soon. Let your leaders go to Caesarea with me and accuse the man if he has done anything wrong."

Festus spent another eight or ten days with them and then went to Caesarea. On the next day he sat down in the court of judgement and ordered Paul to be brought in. When Paul arrived, the Jews who had come from Jerusalem stood round him and started making many serious charges against him, which they were not able to prove. But Paul defended himself: "I have done nothing wrong against the Law of the Jews or against the Temple or against the Roman Emperor."

But Festus wanted to gain favour with the Jews, so he asked Paul, "Would you be willing to go to Jerusalem and be tried on these charges before me there?"

Paul said, "I am standing before the Emperor's own court of judgement, where I should be tried. I have done no wrong to the Jews, as you yourself well know. If I have broken the law and done something for which I deserve the death penalty, I do not ask to escape it. But if there is no truth in the charges they bring against me, no one can hand me over to them. I appeal to the Emperor."

Then Festus, after conferring with his advisers, answered, "You have appealed to the Emperor, so to the Emperor you will go."

Acts 25:22-27

Agrippa said to Festus, "I would like to hear this man myself."

"You will hear him tomorrow," Festus answered.

The next day Agrippa and Bernice came with great pomp and ceremony and entered the audience hall with the military chiefs and the leading men of the city. Festus gave the order, and Paul was brought in. Festus said, "King Agrippa and all who are here with us: You see this man against whom all the Jewish people, both here and in Jerusalem, have brought complaints to me. They scream that he should not live any longer. But I could not find that he had done anything for which he deserved the death sentence. And since he himself made an appeal to the Emperor, I have decided to send him. But I have nothing definite about him to write to the Emperor. So I have brought him here before you – and especially before you, King Agrippa! – so that, after investigating his case, I may have something to write. For it seems unreasonable to me to send a prisoner without clearly indicating the charges against him.'

Acts 26:19-32

"And so, King Agrippa, I did not disobey the vision I had from heaven. First in Damascus and in Jerusalem and then in all Judaea and among the Gentiles, I preached that they must repent of their sins and turn to God and do the things that would show they had repented. It was for this reason that these Jews seized me while I was in the Temple, and they tried to kill me. But to this very day I have been helped by God, and so I stand here giving my witness to all, to small and great alike. What I say is the very same thing which the prophets and Moses said was going to happen: that the Messiah must suffer and be the first one to rise from death, to announce the light of salvation to the Jews and to the Gentiles."

As Paul defended himself in this way, Festus shouted at him, "You are mad, Paul! Your great learning is driving you mad!"

Paul answered, "I am not mad, Your Excellency! I am speaking the sober truth. King Agrippa! I can speak to you with all boldness, because you know about these things. I am sure that you have taken notice of every one of them, for this thing has not happened hidden away in a corner. King Agrippa, do you believe the prophets? I know that you do!"

Agrippa said to Paul, "In this short time do you think you will make me a Christian?"

"Whether a short time or a long time," Paul answered, "my prayer to God is that you and all the rest of you who are listening to me today might become what I am – except, of course, for these chains!"

Then the king, the governor, Bernice, and all the others got up, and after leaving they said to each other, "This man has not done anything for which he should die or be put in prison." And Agrippa said to Festus, "This man could have been released if he had not appealed to the Emperor."

ADDITIONAL BIBLE REFERENCES FOR PRIVATE STUDY

Acts 25:13-21

Acts 26:1-18

BACKGROUND NOTES

1. Procurator Felix

Felix was governor of Palestine from about 52 to 59AD, and all sorts of irregularities are believed to have taken place. He is described by the historian Tacitus in his *Annales* as a bad and cruel governor who *'thought he could commit every sort of iniquity and escape the consequences'*. Following an outbreak of violence where Jews were killed and Felix encouraged the troops to loot the houses of the wealthy, the Jews complained to the emperor, Nero, and Felix was recalled.

A clue to the sorry state of public order in the province at that time can be found in Luke's record that four hundred and seventy soldiers were needed to ensure the prisoner Paul's safety on the route from Jerusalem to Caesarea. He had been arrested following an incident where accusations were made of his defiling the Temple by bringing Gentiles into it. The mob became violent and tried to kill him. General uproar ensued. Formal charges were made before Felix in Caesarea, but the governor found himself in a dilemma and adjourned the proceedings: he could not convict Paul because Lysias, the tribune in charge of the garrison, had not identified any legal offence *(Acts 23:29),* and neither had the other accusers; on the other hand Felix was reluctant to release him for fear of offending the Jews, and because he hoped Paul might offer him a bribe. He therefore decided to postpone the verdict to keep the options open. This state of affairs continued until his removal two years later.

At least Paul had to be kept reasonably comfortable whilst in custody, on account of his status as a Roman citizen, so he was able to come and go with an escort and have contact with his friends. Roman law only permitted prisoners to be held for a maximum of two years, but it is an indication of the corruption of Felix that he was happy to let Paul's captivity continue beyond that time – presumably to please the Jewish leaders. During his imprisonment we know Paul had many discussions with Felix, but there is no evidence that he managed to interest him in the gospel. We can be sure it was not for lack of trying!

2. Procurator Festus

Festus was a very different ruler: a just and upright Roman whose efficient vigour was in sharp contrast with the procrastination of his predecessor. There is no doubt he was greeted with a catalogue of problems at the start of his term of office; this is how the historian Josephus describes the situation in Judaea:

Upon Festus's coming into Judaea, it happened that Judaea was afflicted by the robbers, while all the villages were set on fire, and plundered by them. And then it was that the sicarii, as they were called, who were robbers, grew numerous . . . So Festus sent forces, both horsemen and footmen, to fall upon those that had been seduced by a certain impostor, who promised them deliverance and freedom from the miseries they were under, if they would but follow him as far as the wilderness. Accordingly those forces that were sent destroyed both him that had deluded them, and those that were his followers also. (Antiquities 20.8.10)

Festus was clearly set on restoring peace and harmony to the area, and applied himself speedily to correcting past injustices. The Jews, who tried once or twice to take advantage of him, had little cause for complaint about his administration. Many common criminals were brought to justice, and some semblance of order was restored. Festus was a loyal Roman with the Roman instinct for justice, and he also understood how to use compromise, as can be seen in his treatment of Paul and his accusers and his choice of location for the hearing. Sadly, his term of office was cut short by his death only two years after his appointment. His rule was to be a brief respite for the people, as his two successors were no better than Felix.

The procurator's handling of Paul's case was shrewd and statesmanlike. He dealt with it speedily, travelling to Jerusalem to discuss the charges in person with the Jewish leaders. There is no doubt that he wished to gain their respect, but he stood firm in the face of attempts to manipulate him: he refused to send Paul for trial in Jerusalem, but kept rigidly to the formal Roman procedure. This required that charges were formally prepared, conveyed to the accused, and then heard in the presence of the procurator. This ensured that accuser and accused came face to face in the governor's presence.

The problems began for Festus when he failed to find Paul guilty of any of the charges. These appeared to be religious, and outside his experience if not also his jurisdiction. To keep favour with the Jews, he suggested to Paul that as a compromise he go to stand trial in Jerusalem. When Paul saw the danger and exercised his right to be heard by Nero, Festus was faced with a dilemma: if he could find no guilt, how were charges to be formulated for the emperor? King Agrippa's visit was a timely opportunity for a review of the charges and advice on tactics.

3. King Agrippa

This was King Agrippa II, great-grandson of Herod the Great, and son of King Agrippa I who, according to Luke, was eaten by worms when he offended God *(Acts 12:21-23)*. Agrippa II ruled over a small area of Palestine by permission of the Romans, who had given him the position. Hence the courtesy visit made by him and Queen Bernice at the start of Festus' term of office. He had intimate knowledge of Jewish faith and practice, and was an ideal advisor for the newcomer from Rome. Luke's account suggests that he was respected and appreciated by Romans and Jews alike. He listened to Paul's defence with interest and apparent good humour.

King Agrippa survived the disastrous revolt which occurred only a few years later and killed many of his people; he died in 92AD, bringing the Herodian dynasty to an end. This family, with its pro-Roman policies, had helped to postpone the clash between Rome and the Jews, thus unintentionally preserving the peace also for the early decades of the Christian Church.

4. Paul's defence

Paul made a wise decision when he declined to go to Jerusalem for trial, since the Jewish leaders were planning to murder him on the way. The charges he faced were of heresy, sacrilege and sedition, the last two having been fabricated, and Paul knew that, if he did survive the journey, there would be no chance for him of a fair trial in Jerusalem. To be tried in Rome was a better prospect as the emperor, Nero, was then in the respected Golden Age of his reign. He later persecuted the Christians, but there were as yet no warnings of the unstable behaviour that characterised his later years.

Paul's meeting with King Agrippa was a momentous occasion of high drama, and he prepared his fifth defence speech with care. He had already had to defend himself before the people, the Sanhedrin, Felix and Festus, but this final speech is clearly judged by Luke to be the most important. The scene would have been one of great splendour with the pomp and ceremony of the royal visitors and their entourage, and the governor with his colourful official robes. We are told that military chiefs and the city dignitaries were all in attendance. Festus must have worked quickly to bring them all together in the space of twenty-four hours! Paul, the small, strange-looking tentmaker in his prison chains, must have cut a puny figure before so much pageantry.

Yet in no time he became a commanding presence centre stage, with his scholarly presentation and the inspiration of the Holy Spirit. He recounted his life in its three stages: the years from birth to early adulthood where he followed all the practices of the strict Pharisee; the period when he viciously persecuted his enemies, the Followers of the Way; and finally his years as an apostle commissioned by Jesus himself – Jesus who had died and risen again as the long-awaited Messiah. Not content with his own story, he even cheekily suggested that the king might wish to become a convert!

The total domination of his words can be gauged by the apparent disarray in which he left his judges. They seemed a bewildered company, not quite sure why they were having to judge him at all, and the Holy Spirit seemed to have raised Paul head and shoulders above his distinguished listeners.

DISCUSSION TOPICS

1. Why do we feel suspicious of people who change sides, e.g. in politics?

2. What is the value of compromise? Does it mean we don't have the courage of our convictions? When can it be used profitably in church affairs?

3. What qualities make a good governor or politician? What part can religious belief play?

4. When, if ever, might it be right to disobey or disregard an employer or senior officer?

5. Are you a leader or a behind-the-scenes person? What contribution can both personality types make to a) church b) community?

6. How much are you influenced by appearances – whether regarding people or situations?

7. What problems of Festus' times are still troublesome today? What progress has been made, if any?

8. Was Paul an extremist, as Festus implies? If so, why do we put so much trust in him?

PRAYER

Eternal God,
The light of the minds that know you,
The joy of the hearts that love you,
The strength of the wills that serve you;
Grant us so to know you that we may truly love you,
So to love you that we may truly serve you,
Whom to serve is perfect freedom.

AMEN

(Gelasian Sacramentary)

Paul's journey to Rome

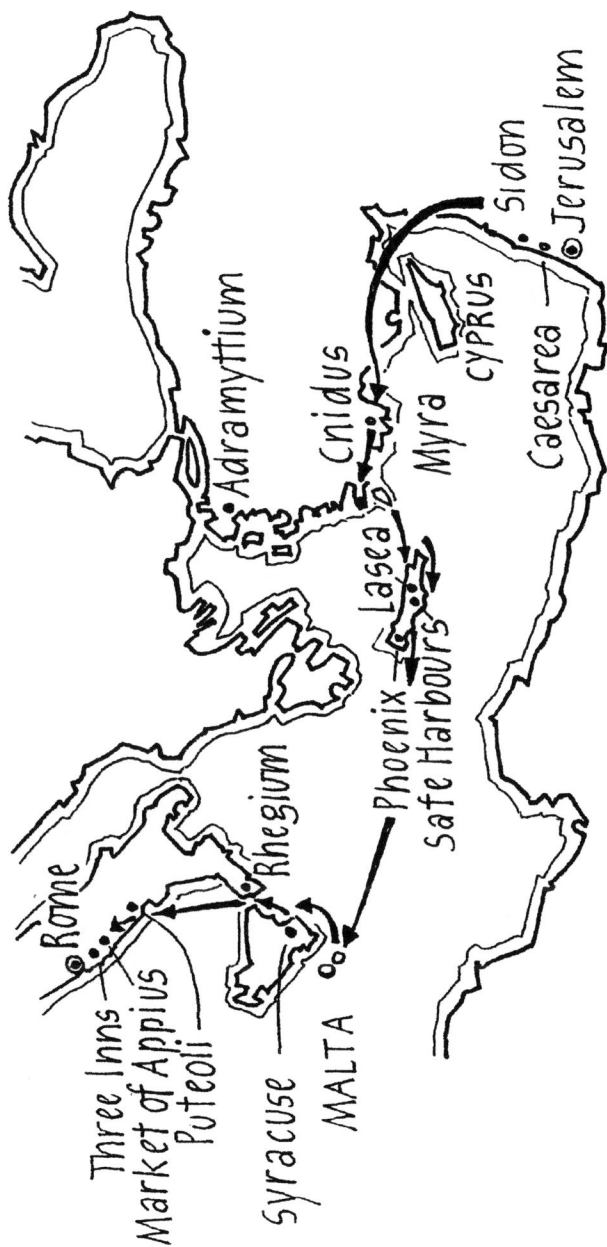

Adramyttium

Cnidus

Myra

CYPRUS

Sidon

Jerusalem

Caesarea

Lasea

Phoenix
Safe Harbours

Rhegium

Rome

Three Inns
Market of Appius
Puteoli

Syracuse

MALTA

PUBLIUS

More visitors! Hello there! And welcome to Malta! I'm Publius, the chief man. If you're looking for a good story, we've certainly got one for you; and you'll like it because this one has a happy ending. But the best part – the most mind-boggling part – is that every word of it's true!

To set the scene I need to tell you a bit about Malta. Although we're quite small, there have been people living here since the Dark Ages – all sorts! It's easy to see why, as we're in a great strategic position for just about everything: merchant vessels or warships can call or shelter here, as our rocky inlets afford splendid protection from the wind, particularly in the north of the island. They come to us from all directions. It's a good place to live, too, with a temperate climate, beautiful scenery and reasonable ground for growing things. So we may be small, but there's always a lot going on.

Somewhere in the distant past the Phoenicians were in charge because it's basically their language we speak. Then eventually the Romans took over, and we've been part of the empire for a couple of centuries. Good they are too, make no mistake, and they've made our lives very comfortable with all their reforms. They rule the high seas, and have made travelling much safer than it used to be, by all accounts. You can see grain ships plying to and fro most weeks in the good months. But, of course, the big enemy is the weather, especially the wind – and there's not a great deal Rome can do about that! So once the autumn sets in, our ships are laid up in the harbour and we all sit tight.

Now that was where the captain of Paul's ship – Julius was his name – made his big mistake: it was too late in the year when he set out for such a long sea journey, and, of course, the winds played havoc from early on. Not that I'm complaining, you understand – if he hadn't taken that gamble, we wouldn't have found out about Jesus Christ! And there isn't a soul on this island would welcome that idea. Life was good enough before, but now it has meaning and purpose, and we're not giving that up in a hurry!

The first inkling we had of Paul and his mates was when a fisherman on the cliff spotted hundreds of tiny figures splashing around out to sea, and heading for our shores – some of them clutching bits of wood. Our coast is very rocky, but there are caves and inlets everywhere in the north, so that was most likely where they were heading. Of course, he couldn't make out what sort of people they were, especially as it was foul weather and the visibility was poor. For all he knew it might have been some sort of invasion. So he grabbed some mates and they rushed down to the shore to meet them. They were able to alert me at once as I've an estate a few miles away, and I was indoors looking after my sick father. We watched them struggling in – hundreds of them – and it was clear they must have come from a big ship. They were a sorry sight, I'm telling you! But my people are a great bunch, and they'd got a huge fire burning even before the first ones came ashore. I think they all made it to safety, and you should have seen the relief on their faces!

Our biggest problem, of course, was trying to talk to them; they didn't speak Malti and I don't know much else. So we contented ourselves with getting them out of the water and up to the fire. They certainly didn't present any sort of threat to us in the state they were in. The chap we came to know as Paul was the one who quickly emerged as a sort of leader, and the others seemed to look to him for guidance. He was a blinking marvel – if you'll pardon the expression – considering what he'd been through. He rushed about helping people and generally making himself useful, and even had a heroic bash at speaking to us – odd words and lots of gestures, you know the sort of thing, but heaven knows where he got the stamina! And then came the first of his miraculous doings. He was stoking the fire yet again when a great snake suddenly appeared from nowhere and locked on to his wrist. We were horrified! What a way to die when you'd just survived a shipwreck! It must be divine retribution for some wickedness, somebody said. But no! With a quick flick, he shook the creature into the fire, apparently unharmed by its hideous fangs! Well, what would you have made of that? My people were convinced he was a god.

We had to forget that for the moment and sort out some hospitality as the poor folk were starving hungry and shivering from their ordeal. My people began to fix them up and I took Paul and some others to my place. I explained about my father's dysentery as I didn't want to expose them to yet more risk, but once again Paul's reaction knocked me sideways. 'Take me to him!' he orders, and so I did. I actually thought he must be a doctor, because he went right up to my father and put his hands on him. I could tell he was praying as he did that and, blow me! before you could count to ten my father sat up energetically as though there was nothing wrong with him. He hadn't sat up for days. That's the honest truth: he was completely cured!

Well, I'm telling you, it got round the island like wildfire! People were so excited that they started bringing sick people from here, there and everywhere. And Paul cured them all – can you believe it? He prayed for

110

every single one of them and they were restored to glowing health! Well, of course, we had to know more about how that could happen, and it's amazing! We could hardly talk to each other and yet in no time we were hearing about Jesus Christ and all that he did for us and for everyone. And his Holy Spirit would still be with us, said Paul, if we repented of our sins and asked for his help. What a story, eh? Now you know what I meant.

It was spring before they were able to resume their journey to Rome, and I've never known a winter pass so quickly. We were sad to see them go, and my people showered them with gifts. But the gift Paul gave to us was more than money can buy, believe you me.

BIBLE PASSAGE

Acts 27:37-44 and Acts 28:1-10

There was a total of 276 of us on board. After everyone had eaten enough, they lightened the ship by throwing all the wheat into the sea.

When day came, the sailors did not recognize the coast, but they noticed a bay with a beach and decided that, if possible, they would run the ship aground there. So they cut off the anchors and let them sink in the sea, and at the same time they untied the ropes that held the steering oars. Then they raised the sail at the front of the ship so that the wind would blow the ship forward, and we headed for shore. But the ship hit a sandbank and went aground; the front part of the ship got stuck and could not move, while the back part was being broken to pieces by the violence of the waves.

The soldiers made a plan to kill all the prisoners, in order to keep them from swimming ashore and escaping. But the army officer wanted to save Paul, so he stopped them from doing this. Instead, he ordered those who could swim to jump overboard first and swim ashore; the rest were to follow, holding on to the planks or to some broken pieces of the ship. And this was how we all got safely ashore.

When we were safely ashore, we learnt that the island was called Malta. The natives there were very friendly to us. It had started to rain and was cold, so they lit a fire and made us all welcome. Paul gathered up a bundle of sticks and was putting them on the fire when a snake came out on account of the heat and fastened itself to his hand. The natives saw the snake hanging on Paul's hand and said to one another, "This man must be a murderer, but Fate will not let him live, even though he escaped from the sea." But Paul shook the snake off into the fire without being harmed at all. They were waiting for him to swell up or suddenly fall down dead. But after waiting for a long time and not seeing anything unusual happening to him, they changed their minds and said, "He is a god!"

Not far from that place were some fields that belonged to Publius, the chief official of the island. He welcomed us kindly and for three days we were his guests. Publius' father was in bed, sick with fever and dysentery. Paul went into his room, prayed, placed his hands on him, and healed him. When this happened, all the other sick people on the island came and were healed. They gave us many gifts, and when we sailed, they put on board what we needed for the voyage.

ADDITIONAL BIBLE REFERENCES FOR PRIVATE STUDY

Acts 19:11-20 (more miracles performed by God through Paul)

Colossians 3:1-17 (the sort of teaching Paul's listeners would receive)

BACKGROUND NOTES

1. Final journey to Rome

The account of Paul's two thousand mile journey to Rome begins at Acts 27:1. He was first of all taken aboard a ship bound for Asia Minor, and this part of the trip was uneventful, although the winds were already picking up. For the next step, the captain found an Egyptian grain vessel bound for Italy, but due to the lateness of the season, this ship met opposition from north-easterly gales and storms as it headed across open sea between Crete and Sicily. It was wrecked near the northern coast of Malta in AD60, and the travellers were forced to wait until spring to resume their journey. Another Egyptian grain ship took them on the final leg of their journey to Puteoli in Italy. From there Paul travelled overland to Rome.

2. Malta

Malta is about eighteen miles long and eight miles wide, and is situated fifty-eight miles south of Sicily and a hundred and eighty miles north and east of the African coast. In the south-west the cliffs drop vertically to the sea, but the northern coast is dotted with caves, bays and inlets. The largest harbour is the site of present-day Valletta, and St. Paul's Bay, the traditional site of the shipwreck, is eight miles further north-west. Here a sandy spit stretches out to sea and could well have caused a struggling vessel to run aground.

There are no rivers but there are sources of water underground and the soil of the island, although shallow, is productive; there would no doubt have been good crops of wheat, olives, figs, grapes and other fruits in Paul's time. Malta is known for its aromatic honey which was probably also enjoyed then.

Archaeological investigations have revealed habitation on Malta as far back as 5000BC when Neolithic farmers arrived there. The Phoenicians colonised the island in the seventh or eighth centuries BC, and gave it the name of Melita, which means 'a place of refuge' or some say 'affording honey'. They also gave it the basis of the Malti language. The next to occupy the island were the Carthaginians, and the language became modified by the Arabic influence of that time. The Romans took over in 218BC and Malta remained part of the empire until the sixth century. In Paul's time it was known both for its prosperity and for its fine architecture. There have been numerous other influences up to the present time so, although a tiny island, Malta is blessed with an extraordinarily colourful history and cultural heritage.

3. Publius

The Roman Empire was reorganised under the emperor, Augustus, and Malta was put under the authority of a governor known as a 'chief' or 'first' man of the island, who seems to have been allowed a fair degree of autonomy in conducting Malta's affairs. Publius, who held the post at the time of the shipwreck, had an estate in or near the Roman city of Melita, which was a sizeable city encompassing the modern towns of Mdina and Rabat. It was situated about five miles from the supposed location of Paul's arrival ashore. We are told that Publius extended hospitality to the travellers for three days, but they are thought to have spent the rest of their stay in caves near Rabat, in the vicinity of the governor's domain.

According to tradition, Publius later became the first Bishop of Malta.

4. Conversion of Malta

Paul was the first to bring news of the gospel to Malta, and Christianity has thrived on the island until the present day. Roman Catholicism has, throughout the centuries, maintained an influence on social, political and even economic issues, and guide books to the island record as recently as 1996 that eighty-seven per cent of Maltese are regular churchgoers, a higher percentage than is found elsewhere in Europe.

When Paul was gripped by the viper as he stoked the beach fire, the locals jumped to the conclusion he was a murderer who was being punished by

Dike, the goddess of vengeance and retribution. So his mastery over the creature left them dumbfounded and inclined to see him as a god, or favourite of the gods. The further healings reported by Luke would reinforce their respect for him, but we can be sure Paul did not leave matters like that: he would have used the winter months to teach them about Jesus Christ, and the Holy Spirit who was the true source of this healing power. The appreciation of the islanders is shown by the gifts bestowed on him when the travellers departed for Rome. Paul must have been greatly encouraged by the way in which God had used the shipwreck for an effective mission to another Gentile community. The power of Paul's ministry had continued so strong throughout this period, that we tend to forget he was a captive *en route* for trial by the Roman emperor.

DISCUSSION TOPICS

1. In what ways could you or your church offer hospitality?

2. How good are we at giving a welcome to foreigners a) as personal friends b) at church c) in our community generally?

3. What evidence would a newcomer see of the Holy Spirit at work in your church?

4. How is a) Christian education b) prayer, organised in your church? How do you personally 'recharge your batteries' for your service as a Christian?

5. What great Christians, alive or dead, have had a particular influence over you?

6. Have you succeeded in a) interesting someone in the gospel b) persuading someone to come along to your church? How did you do this?

7. What different ways can you think of to spread the gospel particularly to children and young people?

8. What sort of work should a Christian missionary do in our world today?

PRAYER

'It is you who are the witnesses to it all' (Luke 24:48 N.E.B.)

Dear Father God, you have called us to be your witnesses for Christ, proclaiming the gospel wherever we go.

We ask you to bless those who serve as missionaries overseas. Equip them with practical skills to benefit their communities; give them endurance to face harsh or hostile conditions; grant them wisdom to convey your love where opportunities occur.

Empower them, Lord, with your Holy Spirit.

You call others to preach and teach the Good News in our own country.

We pray for all who have leadership roles in the Church: ministers, lay preachers, pastors, evangelists, and all with responsibility for young people. May their words inspire a true desire for knowledge and commitment.

Empower them, Lord, with your Holy Spirit.

You call some to care in the community.

We ask you to bless doctors and nurses, the police and emergency services, and all who care for people in need, or relieve suffering. May their love and compassion give a glimpse of the infinite love of your Son, Jesus Christ.

Empower them, Lord, with your Holy Spirit.

Many are called to witness at home, school or work.

Give them courage to express their faith freely, and resolution to put it into practice. May their patience and understanding in relationships work towards peace in the world, and may their selfless love offer a foretaste of your heavenly kingdom.

Empower us all, Lord, with your Holy Spirit.
We ask it for Jesus Christ's sake,

AMEN

LUKE

Good day to you, dear readers! I'm delighted to meet you. I'm Luke, the writer of Acts, and I'm honoured you've stayed with me to the end of the story. But, of course, that's no credit to my writing. What a blockbuster! Have you ever been so moved by a book before? Have your spirits ever been so uplifted from the daily grind? What an antidote for the worries that poison your peace of mind! Has the future ever seemed so rosy? Although I said 'end of the story', of course, it wasn't the end – rather the beginning. When Paul set out on his odyssey, it was like a pressure-cooker gathering steam; the pressure of the gospel built up until the power became so intense that the cooker exploded, and the Good News showered over the Gentile world. Everyone who came into contact with the steam of the Holy Spirit felt its heat.

And it wasn't the end of Paul's story either. We left him in Rome, bracing himself for confrontation with the emperor, but that narrative must be for another writer. **My** purpose was twofold: to chart the journey of Jesus Christ through our world in human form, teaching about the kingdom and finally enduring suffering and death for us before being raised to glory; and then secondly, to chart the spread of the Good News to the Gentile world. I am a Gentile, so who better to be your commentator? My mission was to tell people that the news of the Holy Spirit was already spreading like wildfire – they must grasp it, since it's for everyone. Jesus gave firm instructions that we who were witnesses had this duty to take the message to all nations.

People have asked how I know so much. Some even suggest that if I'm a storyteller I might have made it all up! Believe me, friends, this is not something you make up. For much of Paul's travelling I was there at his side, and after such indelible experiences of God's presence and power, I can assure you I tested the integrity of all my other material. Anything less than the truth would eat at my book like a cancer. The best way to convince you is to recount three occasions when I was there with Paul in the thick of the action. No further evidence is necessary, for no one who stood in my shoes then could be troubled by doubts.

I'll start with our trip to Philippi, which was Paul's second journey. He'd had a dream that someone needed our help in Macedonia, so, assuming it to be a call from God, we set sail as soon as we could fix it. Once over there, we headed for Philippi, and the most vivid memories I have of that visit concern women. I mention that because so often in our time we're guilty of ignoring our ladies and the vital contribution they make to society. For my non-Christian friends they're no more than second-class citizens, but Jesus taught us to think otherwise. It so happened that, on the Sabbath, we were looking for somewhere to pray. On the banks of the river we met this group of Jews – many of them women – enjoying worship together. We joined them, and Paul was soon inspired to speak to them about Jesus. A charming lady called Lydia – a foreign business woman – was quick to respond to his teaching. I'm sure you know the details, but that was a crucial moment in our mission. Lydia not only accepted Jesus into her life, but she put her home at our disposal and in no time it had become the headquarters of the new church of Philippi. God's role was clear for us all to see: he'd guided us to that place with specific prompting, and added Gentiles to our numbers.

There was further excitement for me in that city when Paul cured a demented slave girl. What a poor, tortured wisp of humanity she was! You may know I'm a doctor, so such sights affect me deeply. It also means that I'm well placed to verify the authenticity of such cures. I can assure you there was no doubt in my mind that the girl had been freed from her indisposition, and the healing power was the Holy Spirit. This leads to the second occasion when I observed Paul in action: it was another healing, but one you may not know about.

This time we were in Troas, on Paul's third trip; we'd dined and were enjoying fellowship together one Saturday evening with Timothy and other friends – a relaxing occasion and not the usual material for my histories. If you can picture the scene, we were sitting replete from a hearty meal, somewhat somnolent from the wine, warm from the lamps and the heat of our bodies crowded together, and happy as usual to leave centre stage to Paul. Never at a loss for words, he chatted on till past midnight. Then it happened! A young chap had been perched on the window-sill – Eutychus, his name – I'd not noticed him in the crowd. Presumably tranquillised by the even tones of Paul's voice, he dozed off and hurtled three floors to the ground. I flew out to attend to him, but it was hopeless. No one could survive that. Or so I thought! Paul took charge, and cradled him in his arms, telling us not to worry, all would be well! Within minutes – against all sensible medical probability – he was conscious and demanding nourishment! So you see? Clear proof once again of the Lord at work.

Then my third incident has to be our sea trip to Malta. What drama! What proof of the cataclysmic might of the elements, the miserable frailty of us humans, and then – crowning everything – the omnipotence of God! We were battered night and day by the fury of the gales, our cargo was jettisoned leaving no sustenance for our many passengers, ship's parts were thrown to the waves, and yet we all survived! Paul told us that an angel had guaranteed this. I'm not sure anyone believed him then, but in the course of time we struggled ashore, every single one!

Dear friends, I can think of no better note on which to end. You see, this is the world in microcosm – your world and mine. Day by day it tears itself apart in the storms of life; we thrash around helplessly, seizing opportunities but caving in under strains; our eyes are dimmed by the fog of uncertainty; we don't know where we're going ... until we remember that we are held in God's hand, and he has promised to bring us safely ashore.

Farewell, and God speed!

BIBLE PASSAGES

Acts 1:1-5

Dear Theophilus:
In my first book I wrote about all the things that Jesus did and taught from the time he began his work until the day he was taken up to heaven. Before he was taken up, he gave instructions by the power of the Holy Spirit to the men he had chosen as his apostles. For 40 days after his death he appeared to them many times in ways that proved beyond doubt that he was alive. They saw him, and he talked with them about the Kingdom of God. And when they came together, he gave them this order: "Do not leave Jerusalem, but wait for the gift I told you about, the gift my Father promised. John baptized with water, but in a few days you will be baptized with the Holy Spirit."

Acts 20:6-12

We sailed from Philippi after the Festival of Unleavened Bread, and five days later we joined them in Troas, where we spent a week.

On Saturday evening we gathered together for the fellowship meal. Paul spoke to the people and kept on speaking until midnight, since he was going to leave the next day. Many lamps were burning in the upstairs room where we were meeting. A young man named Eutychus was sitting in the window, and as Paul kept on talking, Eutychus got sleepier and sleepier, until he finally went sound asleep and fell from the third storey to the ground. When they picked him up, he was dead. But Paul went down and threw himself on him and hugged him. "Don't worry," he said, "he is still alive!" Then he went back upstairs, broke bread, and ate. After talking with them for a long time, even until sunrise, Paul left. They took the young man home alive and were greatly comforted.

Acts 27:14-26

But soon a very strong wind – the one called "North-Easter" – blew down from the island. It hit the ship, and since it was impossible to keep the ship headed into the wind, we gave up trying and let it be carried along by the wind. We got some shelter when we passed to the south of the little island of Cauda. There, with some difficulty, we managed to make the ship's boat secure. They pulled it aboard and then fastened some ropes tight round the ship. They were afraid that they might run into the sandbanks off the coast of Libya, so they lowered the sail and let the ship be carried by the wind. The violent storm continued, so on the next day they began to throw some of the ship's cargo overboard, and on the following day they threw part of the ship's equipment overboard. For many days we could not see the sun or the stars, and the wind kept on blowing very hard. We finally gave up all hope of being saved.

After those on board had gone a long time without food, Paul stood before them and said, "Men, you should have listened to me and not have sailed from Crete; then we would have avoided all this damage and loss. But now I beg you, take heart! Not one of you will lose your life; only the ship will be lost. For last night an angel of the God to whom I belong and whom I worship came to me and said, 'Don't be afraid, Paul! You must stand before the Emperor. And God in his goodness to you has spared the lives of all those who are sailing with you.' So take heart, men! For I trust in God that it will be just as I was told. But we will be driven ashore on some island."

ADDITIONAL BIBLE REFERENCES FOR PRIVATE STUDY

Acts 27:27-44

Acts 28:16-31

BACKGROUND NOTES

1. Luke

Luke was the only Gentile of the New Testament writers, a doctor by profession (*'Luke, our dear doctor'*, *Colossians 4:14)*, and a fluent speaker of idiomatic Greek. He is the patron saint of doctors, and, as one might expect, his writing reveals this special interest by numerous references to medical matters: the scales falling from Saul's eyes after his conversion; the food needed to regain his strength; the distress of the demented slave girl; the healing of the Maltese governor's father, and many others.

Luke is also patron saint of artists, as his many talents are believed to have included painting. He was a highly educated man, a reliable historian and a gifted writer. Scholars comment on his artistry of language, meticulous organisation of his material, and huge vocabulary. His books are said to include hundreds of words not found elsewhere in the New Testament. They are also agreed on his remarkable accuracy of detail, seen for instance in the technical seafaring terminology evoking the storm in Acts 27. Luke clearly enjoyed travel, particularly by sea.

Another characteristic evident in his writing is his warm interest in people, notably Gentiles, women, sick people and the poor or underprivileged.

The Book of Acts was probably written in the early or mid-sixties AD, as there is no mention of Nero's persecutions, the Jewish revolt of AD66, or Paul's death in about 67AD. Luke's purpose in writing his two books was to record an accurate account of the facts about Christianity *(Luke 1:1-4)*, to replace the rumour that abounded. Luke's two books are the only New Testament books to be dedicated to a patron, Theophilus, although the practice was common in the Graeco-Roman world. Theophilus may have been a wealthy aristocrat or possibly just a pseudonym for all devout Gentiles interested in the writing. Luke's particular aim was to set the record straight about the spread of the gospel to the Gentiles, and he was also keen to reassure people that the Christians were not a subversive influence for the Roman Empire. He quotes several occasions when Roman officials could find no fault with Paul and his activities.

Luke's two books trace the story of Christ's kingdom from its heralding by John the Baptist to its proclamation by Paul in Rome, the heart of the empire. Towards the end of the final chapter, Luke quotes Paul saying, *'You are to know, then, that God's message of salvation has been sent to the Gentiles.'* That accomplished, his writing task was fulfilled.

Luke is believed to have remained unmarried throughout his life, and died at the age of eighty-four.

2. The 'we' sections in Acts

There are three sections of the Acts when Luke in his narrative changes the pronoun from 'he' or 'they' to 'we', and this is taken to denote a period when the writer was himself present in the action.

The first is Acts 16:10-18. It begins with Paul's vision of the Macedonian summoning him for help. Scholars suggest the Macedonian may have been Luke himself. There is also a suggestion that the reason for Luke's participation in the journey may have been that Paul was in poor health at that time, and welcomed the presence of his doctor friend. The obstacle to their activity seen as the will of the Spirit *(Acts 16:7)* may have been a euphemism for a spell of illness which put Paul temporarily out of action.

Luke accompanied Paul to Philippi where he witnessed the incident with the disturbed slave girl, but the two men had parted company by the time Paul was released from prison and continued on his travels.

The second 'we' section is Acts 20:5 - 21:18. It begins with Luke sailing from Philippi, where he had probably stayed since Paul's departure, to join Paul in Troas, where they met others for a fellowship meal. The account is more detailed at this point, probably because Luke had firsthand information. Paul resumed the journey on his own by land, but then the men were together for the last stage of his third journey, a sea trip to Ephesus via certain Greek island locations, a meeting with the elders of Ephesus to bid them farewell, and finally a sea trip to Jerusalem with several breaks where they enjoyed the hospitality of various Christian communities. Luke mentions how, at the home of Philip the Evangelist, they all tried to dissuade Paul from returning to Jerusalem, but in vain. Once in Jerusalem the two men met James, leader of the church, and all the elders.

The final 'we' section is Acts 27:1 - 28:16.

When after two years imprisonment in Caesarea, governor Festus sent Paul to Rome, Luke was again in attendance. Once in Rome Luke remained with him and may well have used this period for his writing.

3. Luke's sources

1. His own diary of the three occasions when he was present with Paul.

2. His close friendship with Paul, and all the experiences they shared, must have provided firsthand information and an intimate knowledge of the apostle.

3. The deacon, Philip, in whose house they had stayed, would have furnished information about the early years of the Christian mission – as no doubt would other witnesses of the coming of the Holy Spirit at Pentecost.

4. Records, either verbal or written, from the local churches.

4. The Holy Spirit

The Holy Spirit is the brightly-coloured thread which runs throughout the Book of Acts, and yet it is quite difficult to work out who or what the Holy Spirit actually is. So what clues can we glean from Luke to help us on our way? What are the attributes of the Holy Spirit?

i) He is a divine person for whom the personal pronoun 'he' is always used (although there is some evidence in the Christian tradition for female descriptions of the Holy Spirit). He has the power of speech, he can direct people, he devises and forbids courses of action, and he appoints people to office in the church.

ii) He is the gift promised to the disciples by the risen Jesus, and he made himself known to the believers very powerfully in wind and fire at Pentecost. As they became filled with the Spirit, they were granted new powers of communication and commitment for the Lord's mission.

iii) He has the power to bind people together and overcome division (*Acts 19:1-7*).

iv) He is a vital ingredient for the life, work and growth of every church (*Acts 9:31*)

v) He is in everyone who comes to Christ seeking forgiveness and salvation.

DISCUSSION TOPICS

1. What clues can you detect of Luke's profession of doctor?

2. In what different ways can writing be used to spread the gospel worldwide?

3. How would you defend the authenticity of Luke's account (if indeed you **would** defend it!) to people who have doubts?

4. What do you think of the way events are reported in the media nowadays? What comments might Luke have made?

5. What insights have you gained from your study of Acts? How important would you consider this book for the teaching of Christianity?

6. Did you find any incident particularly moving or disturbing?

7. In Luke's day race, class and gender were divisive issues. How have they changed?

8. Has your church a clear, active and continuing policy of mission? Are you involved?

PRAYER

Finish then thy new creation,
Pure and spotless let us be;
Let us see thy great salvation,
Perfectly restored in thee:
Changed from glory into glory,
Till in heaven we take our place,
Till we cast our crowns before thee,
Lost in wonder, love, and praise!

Charles Wesley (1707 - 88)

BIBLIOGRAPHY

Atlas of the Bible, Reader's Digest, 1983.

William Barclay, *A Beginner's Guide to the New Testament,* Saint Andrew Press, 1992.

William Barclay, *The Acts of the Apostles,* Saint Andrew Press, 1979.

William Barclay, *Corinthians,* Saint Andrew Press, 1982.

William Barclay, *God's Young Church,* Saint Andrew Press, 1970.

William Barclay, *Philippians, Colossians and Thessalonians,* Saint Andrew Press, 1987.

William Barclay, *Romans,* Saint Andrew Press, 1978.

Black and Rowley, eds., *Peake's Commentary on the Bible,* Nelson, 1964.

E. M. Blaiklock, *Today's Handbook of Bible Characters,* Bethany House, 1979.

A. C. Bouquet, *Everyday Life in New Testament Times,* Batsford, 1954.

Robert Boyd, *Paul the Apostle,* World Bible, 1995.

Ronald Brownrigg, *Who's Who in the New Testament,* Dent, 1993.

Donald Coggan, *Meet Paul,* Triangle, 1998.

William L. Coleman, *Today's Handbook of Bible Times and Customs,* Bethany House, 1984.

Thomas Cook, *Traveller's Malta and Gozo,* 1996.

The Encyclopedia of the Bible, Lion, 1978.

Good News Bible, special edition in full colour with features by Lion, the Bible Society, 1976.

Handbook to the Bible, Lion, 1976.

The History of Christianity, Lion, 1977.

The Interpreter's Dictionary of the Bible, Abingdon Press, 1990.

Jesus and his Times, Reader's Digest 1987.

Josephus, *Works,* trans. William Whiston Hendrickson, 2001.

Herbert Lockyer, *All the Men of the Bible,* Zondervan, 1958.

Herbert Lockyer, *All the Women of the Bible,* Zondervan, 1967.

Richard N. Longenecker, *Expositor's Bible Commentary – Acts,* Zondervan, 1995.

The Oxford Dictionary of the Christian Church, ed. F. L. Cross, revised Cross and Livingstone Oxford University Press, 1990.

Packer, Tenney and White, *Marshall's Bible Handbook,* Marshall, Morgan and Scott, 1980.

J. B. Phillips, *Letters to Young Churches,* Geoffrey Bles, 1956.

J. B. Phillips, *The Young Church in Action,* Geoffrey Bles, 1955.

David Robinson, ed,. *Concordance to the Good News Bible,* British and Foreign Bible Society, 1983.

John Stott, revised Stephen Motyer, *Men with a Message,* Candle Books, 1997.

John R. W. Stott, *The Message of Acts,* Inter-Varsity Press, 1991.

Frances Young, The Significance of John Wesley's Conversion Experience in *John Wesley: Contemporary Perspectives,* Epworth Press, 1988.

ACKNOWLEDGEMENTS

All Scripture quotations, except those in the Introduction and the prayer relating to Silas, are from the *Good News Bible* published by the Bible Societies/HarperCollins Publishers Ltd. U. K. copyright American Bible Society, 1966, 1971, 1976, 1992, and are used with the permission of the publishers.

The quotation of Luke 24:47-48 used in the Introduction is taken from the New English Bible, copyright the British and Foreign Bible Society 1972 and 1992. Used by permission.

The quotation of Psalm 111 is taken from the HOLY BIBLE, NEW INTERNATIONAL VERSION. Copyright © 1973, 1978, 1984 by International Bible Society. Used by permission.

The Methodist Covenant Prayer is used by permission of the Trustees for Methodist Church Purposes.

Thanks, as ever, to my husband-in-a-million, John, and to the Revd. Eric Maynard, for correction of my work and suggestions for improvement.

Thank you to my daughter, Liz Wickens, for proofreading and editorial comment.